Before '9
of the 1978-79 New York Rangers

Mark Rosenman and Howie Karpin

Foreword by Dave Maloney

Copyright © 2019 Mark Rosenman and Howie Karpin

All rights reserved.

ISBN:9780692189283

DEDICATION

To the 32 men who put on a Rangers jersey during the 1978–79 season and took us on a wild ride to the Stanley Cup Finals. And to Marv Albert, Sal "Red Light" Messina, Jim Gordon, and "The Big Whistle" Bill Chadwick, who painted the picture for us all.

CONTENTS

	Foreword	5
1	From Fergy to Freddie: The Stage is Set	11
2	Sudden Death, Sudden Birth	18
3	"The Frank Sinatra Song"	23
4	The Fog Lifts the Rangers	28
5	The Youngest Captain	34
6	October: Fast Start	39
7	November: Building an Identity	46
8	December: Gettin' Busy	56
9	January: Murder in the First	69
10	February: "Potvin Sucks"	79
11	March/April: Headin' Towards the Playoffs	92
12	Preliminary Round: Step One	105
13	Quarterfinals: Freddie's Revenge	111
14	SemiFInal: The Battle For New York	123
15	Stanley Cup Finals: Coming Up Short	144
16	Epilogue: "Woulda, Coulda, Shoulda	154
17	Where Are They Now	157
	Acknowledgements	168

FOREWORD BY DAVE MALONEY

It is one of the moments of that enchanted playoff spring of 1979 that stands out in memory. It was late in the second period of Game 5 at the Forum in Montreal where we had been pinned in our end of the ice for what now seems like forever when Jacques Lemaire finally put the puck in our net to make the score 4-1 in favor of the Canadiens. As we were heading to the bench my partner on defense Carol Vadnais, God rest his wonderful soul, gasped, " Thank goodness they scored. Now we are finally out of our end!" For all intents and purpose our glorious, unsuspecting Stanley Cup run was over. And what a run it was.

From the back pages of the Post and Daily News, to the front page of the Times to whooping it up at Studio 54, you name it we were the toast of the Big Apple. We know how it ended, but how did it all start? Who knows? I am not sure anyone can truly say how this really good mix of veteran and youth came within three games of capturing the Stanley Cup. I guess like a lot of surprising stories, things just seem to fall into place and happen.

To kick things off Fred Shero was hired as coach and general manager following the preceding season. Brought over from the Flyers with a couple of cups on his resume I am not sure what we expected from the guy whose teams had basically pounded their opponents into submission on their way to those championships. I do know that if the terms cerebral, thoughtful and perhaps even unassuming had been used to describe Freddie's influence and demeanor I for one would have been totally shocked! In those days the Flyers were far from being cerebral, thoughtful and unassuming!

With their first pick in the 1978 amateur draft the Rangers selected my brother Don. Recalled from the AHL in February Don would be a perfect fit on a line of Phil and the two Dons. Of course, Phil being future Hall of Famer Phil Esposito and the other Don, the mercurially talented Don Murdoch. Brother Don would establish rookie playoff scoring records, something I am sure he dreamt about doing while growing up on the ponds of Lindsay Ontario. To this day I relish the closeness I have with Don largely as a result of our time together on the Rangers. A guy could not have been prouder of his younger brother.

Ulf Nilsson and Anders Hedberg had that special summer day when Garden president Sonny Werblin in his true impresario fashion had the ice lain at MSG to introduce these two wonderful Swedes who were to bring their creative, brave games to Broadway from the WHA. Unfortunately Ulf's season and ultimately his career were severely compromised when he was hit and injured, by the Islanders Denis Potvin, in a regular season game. That event lives in Ranger infamy with the "Potvin Sucks!" chant that we hear even today. We sure missed Ulf in the spring.

The absolute backbone of our run was the play of John Davidson. Acquired from St. Louis in 1975, JD was the key both on and off the ice. His athletic, uber competitive game belied his size. To me he was a bigger version of the guy who would in 1994 backstop the Ranger franchise to a Cup win, Mike Richter. Battling injury down the stretch to this day I believe, had JD been 100% healthy our Cup chase may very well have ended differently in '79. Just as significant was JD's impact in the locker room. He connected with everyone, from the training staff, to the players, to the coaches. As time moved on, in a first in league history the Vancouver Canucks would name their goaltender, Roberto Luongo captain. From my perspective JD could have easily been the first goaltender captain long before Luongo was the first!

Growing organically and developing from within play significant roles on any road to success. A lot of times the work of those on the ground floor gets lost when the story gets closer to the upper floors of success. The fingerprints of drafting by the staffs of the preceding general managers Emile Francis and John Ferguson are all over that final Ranger roster of 1979. There were 12 Blueshirt draft picks skating in the final series against Montreal. From Steve "Sarge" Vickers in '71, thru brother Don in '78 The Cat and Fergie did some job laying the groundwork for what happened come springtime.

Besides Don and Sarge those draft picks included Pat "Disco Hitch" Hickey, Ron "Gresh" Greschner, Eddie "Ciggie" Johnstone, "Murder" Murdoch, Dave "Omar" Farrish, Mike "Q" McEwen, Ron "Doogs" Duguay, Lucien "Lootsie" Deblois, Mario Marios, and yours truly. There is no question that the spirit and exuberance that would come to define our team rested in the hands of this group of young home grown Blueshirts.

Gresh's wonderful puck handling and calmness under fire would see him and Sarge outlast us all on Broadway. They would be the only two who would spend their whole career skating in Ranger Blue. Ciggie became a "Blue Seat" favorite with a willing, physical style. Doc was one of the top three best goal-scorers I would ever play with and unfortunately had an NHL career that was shorter than it should have been. Doog's off-ice personae and reputation while certainly well earned belied a speedy, talented on-ice game. "Q" would eventually take his offensive game and tremendous one-time slapper to the Island and win a couple of Cups with those truly great Islander teams. Lootsie and Mario brought fun and a terrific blend of French Canadien passion for and love of hockey to the mix. Omar was one of the games best open-ice hitters whose locker room imitations of opponents kept things loose during the tense times. Disco Hitch, was nicknamed for his despise of disco music and love of country and the outdoors. His 34 goals led the team in goal scoring during the regular season. A great group of guys the elder statesman being Hitch who was all of 25 years old.

It was all fine and dandy to be young and play with youthful exuberance both on and off the ice but the influence of the veterans Espo, Vad and Walter Tkachuk cannot go unmentioned. Both Phil and Carol had won a Cup with the Bruins and besides Sarge; Walter was the only guy left from those really good Ranger teams who came oh-so-close the early '70's. We had a committee of six-seven players that represented a nice cross-section of the team that met for lunch every month or so with assistant coach Mike Nykoluk. The meetings were bit unusual in those days another Freddie assertion I am certain, but these get togethers were a pretty effective way to keep all hands on deck. I know that my role as captain would not have had any chance of without the support of the elder statesmen of the team and this group of lunchers.

I would be remiss in not recognizing the contributions of Dean Talafous, Pierre Plante, Staten Island's own Nick Fotiu and netminders Wayne Thomas and Doug Soetart. Each over the course of a long regular season played an important role. Nicky kept everybody and I mean everybody opponents and teammates alike on their toes. During those times when I was his roommate on the road I had to sleep with one eye open just to make sure he wasn't up the some sort of fun-loving hijinks! All kidding aside Nick may have been one of the best all-round athletes I have ever come across. While his story is a pretty good one, had he had the opportunity to grow up in the hockey world of Canada his NHL career may have had a dramatically different look.

One rather late addition to the tale was that of Bobby Sheehan. And what an addition he was. After losing to the Flyers in the opening game of the second round, "She-Cat" was recalled from the AHL to counter the speed and feistiness of Philly's Ken Linesman. He came with quite a reputation for extra-circular activities but boy did he turn that Flyer series around. He added that extra touch of quickness and agitation that was needed to upend the physically arrogant bullies from Broad Street. During any teams' Stanley Cup run there is a story or two that seems to come out of nowhere. Bobby Sheehan's was one of those stories.

Most of the games of that season and even the playoffs run together and get a bit hazy in memory. I certainly remember blowing out the Kings in the first round opener and beating them in OT in the second game of the best of three series. The Flyers would try and run us out of the building in the second series but couldn't get the goaltending needed to backstop the numerous penalties they would take as a result of their belligerent play. The Islander series was magic on to it's own. The memory of J.P. Parises' OT goal that put the nail in the Rangers 1975 playoff coffin was still pretty raw in Rangeland. The city was abuzz. The weather was springtime warm. It was awesome. The tension surrounding game six was smothering. Goals by Gresh and Doc led us to a 2-1 victory and we booked our ticket to Montreal for the finals.

A win in game one in Montreal. Down goes netminder Bunny Laraque during warm-ups in game two to be replaced by a struggling Ken Dryden who would quickly find his game despite giving up two quick goals. Our early 2-0 lead disappears when the Habs scored six consecutive times. To me, that was when the worm turned. A Hall of Fame loaded Canadiens club was on their way to rolling to a fourth consecutive Stanley Cup victory. A 4-1 loss back at MSG for game three. Game four also at the Garden, ended in an OT loss and the climb very quickly got a lot steeper. And it all ends where the series started, in Montreal in game 5. Game, set, match.

Although the disappointment would be as expected when you get that close and don't win I do remember feeling how abruptly it did all seem to end. Talk about a feeling of emptiness. Just like that it was over. We had fallen three games short. You endure all the work, sweat, practice, travel, laughs, fights, goals, saves, injuries, and all those things that are part and parcel of a long NHL season and just like that it's done. I won't speak for my teammates but I did believe that this group would surely get another shot at it but we never did. It was not long before I came to realize how hard it was to be the last team standing. The Herb Brooks teams of the 80's were pretty good. But pretty good wasn't good enough to beat the dynasty bound Islanders. In '79 we were that close. Three games. Boy…

Despite all that I would not trade in the experience, memories or relationships garnered along the way for anything in the world. It was a wonderful ride one I would jump aboard again in a nanosecond. Although come to think of it maybe, just maybe we could make the outcome just a bit different. Like finding three more ways to win!

Mark and Howie will take it from here. Their extensive research, their tracking down and interviewing of so many of the guys who made the story what it was will allow those who lived it to take a trip down memory lane. Myself included. For those who weren't around here's to hoping there is enjoyment to be found in the saga of a magical season when a core of young guys backstopped by spectacular goaltending, led a small but wily group of veterans and a mystical coach took The Big Apple on a joyous pursuit of hockey's holy grail. The Stanley Cup.

—Dave Maloney

CHAPTER 1
FROM FERGY TO FREDDIE: THE STAGE IS SET

The New York Rangers' run to the 1979 Stanley Cup Finals actually began before the 1977–78 season when then–general manager John Ferguson named Jean Guy Talbot as their new head coach.

In January 1976, Ferguson was hired for a dual role, replacing Emile Francis as general manager and Ron Stewart as the head coach. After posting a 43–59–19 record in a year and a half behind the bench, Ferguson, to no one's surprise, handed the head coaching reins to Talbot, his assistant during the 1976–77 season.

The Rangers were a perennial Stanley Cup contender in the early 1970s but disappointed their fans by coming up short each year. After losing to the Boston Bruins in six games in the 1972 Stanley Cup Finals, they suffered a crushing defeat in the 1975 playoffs when they lost to the upstart New York Islanders who were only in their third season in the National Hockey League.

In the third and deciding game of the preliminary round at Madison Square Garden, the Islanders beat the Rangers, 4–3, in overtime on J.P. Parise's goal just 11 seconds into the extra session. The loss set the tone for the rivalry between the teams and began a ripple effect that was felt throughout the Rangers organization.

Francis left the bench and named Stewart as the head coach in 1975–76, but both were gone halfway through the season when

Ferguson took over. Talbot was named the head coach on August 22, 1977, but he was already facing an uphill battle. Ten days prior, promising young right wing Don Murdoch was arrested in Toronto for cocaine possession.

Murdoch had burst on the NHL scene in October 1976 as a 20-year-old when he tied a Rangers rookie record with a five-goal game in a 10–4 rout of the North Stars in Minnesota. The flashy right wing had 30 goals in 43 games and was on his way to breaking the NHL record for goals by a rookie when disaster struck in February 1977. During a practice, Murdoch suffered torn tendons in his left ankle when his skate got caught in the boards. The freak injury cost him a shot at the record. He ended up with 32 goals and finished second in the voting to Atlanta's Willi Plett for the Calder Trophy as the league's top rookie.

Going into the 1977–78 season, Talbot and the Rangers felt they had a budding star to team with captain Phil Esposito, a future Hall of Famer, but the consequences of Murdoch's arrest would not be felt until the next offseason (see Chapter 4).

The Rangers got off to a slow start in 1977–78. After ten games, they were 4–5–1 and they would never see .500 for the remainder of the season.

The Rangers could never really get going under Talbot, who indicated that he could not get "the room" onto the same page. "I could not bring them together as a team," Talbot said. "Phil [Esposito] and Rod [Gilbert] did not get along, it was a bad locker room at times, lots of yelling and screaming, then Murdoch's injury hurt us as well as he was well on his way to a 30-goal season." Murdoch injured his back in January and later suffered a dislocated left shoulder. There were reports that Gilbert did not get along with Esposito because he was still bitter over the trade that sent his good friend Jean Ratelle to the Boston Bruins.

It did not go well for Gilbert. Nineteen games into the season, the team's all-time leading scorer with 406 goals was "forced" to retire. The 36-year-old was heading into the final year of a three-year deal and he wanted the team to pick up a two-year option on his contract. When that didn't happen, Gilbert staged a 10-day holdout in training camp which proved to be his downfall. He did not score a goal until the 17th game.

Ferguson reportedly told confidants that the 18-year veteran was "contributing to the team's malaise." On Thanksgiving Eve, the Rangers announced they would fulfill all existing contractual arrangements, but Gilbert would no longer play for the team. "Kinda new management sided with Esposito and that's why Rod retired," according to former Ranger Nick Fotiu.

It wasn't an amicable parting and some of Gilbert's teammates took notice. Steve Vickers felt Gilbert got a raw deal from Ferguson. "He was forced out, no question about that," Vickers said. "It wasn't a good dressing room at the time." The move affected the team's camaraderie. "The two big names [Esposito and Gilbert] weren't the best of buddies, no question about that," said Vickers. "It boiled over a little bit into the dressing room."

Fotiu was in the room and could not ignore what was going on. "There was bullshit between Rod and Phil," he said, "but you knew that when you got a guy like Phil and you got a guy like Rod and it's two trains going head to head, you know on the same track, so you knew what was going to happen."

After a 2–2 tie with the Buffalo Sabres at the Garden on New Year's Eve, the Rangers were a disappointing 12–16–9.

The Rangers were fortunate in that they were in a relatively weak Clarence Campbell Conference that season, so even though they were not playing that well, they still had a good chance to qualify for the preliminary round of the Stanley Cup playoffs.

After a wild 7–7 tie on the road against the Minnesota North Stars in March, the Rangers played their best hockey of the season as they went on a season high five-game winning streak. Unfortunately, they followed that up with five straight losses before ending the regular season with a 3–2 win at the Garden against the Chicago Black Hawks, who already clinched the Smythe Division championship and had nothing to play for.

The Rangers ended the 1977–78 season with 83 points (30–37–13) and finished fourth in the Patrick Division but they made the playoffs and would meet the Buffalo Sabres in a best two-of-three series.

Despite qualifying for the postseason, Talbot's job status was tenuous. "It comes with the territory," he said. In December 1977, noted sports executive Sonny Werblin was named the chairman of Madison Square Garden. Running the Rangers was part of Werblin's responsibilities so on the heels of a disappointing season, changes were in order.

Rumors of a replacement had already surfaced and names such as the Montreal Canadiens' Scotty Bowman and the Philadelphia Flyers' Fred Shero, who had both won multiple Stanley Cups, were being reported by the local media. Shero was reportedly looking for a way out of Philadelphia at season's end.

The Rangers' preliminary round opponent was the Buffalo Sabres, who were second in the Adams Division of the Prince of Wales Conference with 105 points.

Talbot made a controversial move in Game 1 when he started Wayne Thomas in goal over the younger John Davidson, who had clearly outplayed the veteran during the regular season. "I had J.D. in the minors and in St. Louis," Talbot said. "I just felt it would have been unfair to start him in game one, he was so inexperienced at the time, so I went with Wayne Thomas."

It proved to be a mistake. Thomas gave up four goals and the Rangers dropped the opening game in Buffalo, 4–1. Talbot would not totally admit he made a mistake but, to his credit, he was open to a change. "After the first game we had a meeting with the goalies and John [GM Ferguson] and we went with J.D. who had a tremendous game in Game 2, and we lost in the third game, but I still think it was right to start Wayne Thomas in the first game," he said.

Looking back, Davidson had no regrets about the decision made by Talbot. "You always want to play because you want to be the guy," he said. "That's just what it is, and so you wait your turn."

In Game 2, Murdoch scored a goal at 1:37 of overtime to give the Rangers an exciting 4–3, sudden death win at the Garden to even the series. Both teams had potential game-winning goals waved off in overtime before Murdoch extended the series to a third game. Murdoch said Phil Esposito made a speech between the third period and overtime to help the team relax. "He said who's gonna be that hero type of thing, who's going to win this," Murdoch said. "He was basically trying to say who's gonna step up and be the hero for us."

One of Davidson's favorite expressions when he became a broadcaster was "Oh Baby." During Game Two, a pair of Rangers fans in the stands became proud parents after Dr. Martin Grossman's pregnant wife went into labor (see Chapter 2).

The season ended with a 4–1 loss in Game 3 and so did Werblin's faith in his management team. "Ferguson and Talbot didn't seem to know what the problem was," Werblin said. "That's because I think they were the problem."

Ferguson was taken aback by the decision to let him go. "I was shocked," he told the Canadian Press. "Obviously anybody who's a coach or GM is eligible to be fired. I knew that, but I thought it only happened if you were doing a bad job. In my case nobody ever told me the reason."

Even though it didn't end well for Ferguson, he had set the foundation for what was to come in the very next season. John Ferguson Jr. said that his father had no regrets. "He believed in the guys he hired, he believed in the people he drafted and developed," Ferguson Jr. said.

Werblin had a plan and it involved three significant figures who would make a huge difference in 1978–79.

John Ferguson always believed in the people he drafted and developed.
(Ralston-Purina Company, makers of Chex cereals [Public domain], via Wikimedia Commons)

CHAPTER 2
SUDDEN DEATH, SUDDEN BIRTH

The overtime win in Game 2 against the Sabres was clearly the most memorable game of the 1977–78 season, but an extraordinary and blissful event that took place off the ice that night provided a memorable moment for a pair of devoted Rangers fans.

Dr. Martin Grossman had been a Rangers season ticket holder since 1964. His wife, Arlene, was pregnant and according to her doctor, was not due for another two weeks. So the couple did what they always did on the night of a home game. Dr. Grossman would drive from his dental practice in Brooklyn to the Garden, while Arlene would take the Long Island Railroad from their home in Roslyn, Long Island, and meet at their seats in Section 336.

Arlene had a lot on her mind that day, which may explain the fact that while she was on the LIRR, she realized her ticket was on the kitchen table in Roslyn. "The funny thing was that I get onto the train, going to the Garden, without a ticket and when I got to the Garden, I was very much pregnant, and very, very, fat."

Mrs. Grossman would have to talk her way into the game so she approached the ticket taker and "I explained to him that I forgot my ticket at home and he looked at me and he said, 'Lady, anyone in your condition wouldn't come to a game like this without a ticket' and he says, 'Go ahead.' So he let me in without a ticket."

Arlene joined her husband and fellow Rangers fans in Section 336 to settle in and enjoy the game. Towards the end of the first period, Arlene would end up seeing her last Rangers goal of the season when Pat Hickey scored the game-tying goal as 17,500 screaming fans got to their feet. "When everyone got up and started screaming after Hickey scored to tie it up," Arlene Grossman said, "I got up then to scream too, but for different reasons." Dr. Grossman looked at his wife and simply said, "You're not going to do this to me now are you?"

Based on what her doctor had told her, Arlene felt she just needed to go to the restroom. "I went into hard labor in the ladies' room and I was very lucky," she said. "There was an attendant there and I told the attendant, please get my husband immediately, and she was smarter than I was. So she went to get the doctor. In the meantime, she sent someone to locate Dr. Grossman, who was at his seat."

Dr. Grossman recalled a security guard coming up to him and asking, "Are you Dr. Grossman? I said 'Yes.' They said, 'Please come with us because your wife's in the ladies' room and she's not feeling well,' and I said, 'Well, they're about to begin the third [sic] period.' So I got up and he says, 'You better take your coat with you,' and that's when I realized that there was something more going on here, more than that she wasn't feeling well and so I took my coat and the next thing I knew they were taking her on a gurney right downstairs."

While heading downstairs on the elevator, Arlene recalled a short conversation between the doctor and her husband. "The doctor said this is going to be fast 'cause she's crowning, and my husband said, 'Does that mean I'm not going to see the rest of the game?'"

When the elevator doors opened, they went to the doctor's

office which happened to be right next to the Rangers' dressing room. Dr. Grossman said, "Arlene proceeded to let out with some profanities, which embarrassed everybody, but nevertheless, it was about twenty minutes or so and then she gave birth to a baby girl. On top of that, this was all going on during the intermission, so all the players were looking in, wondering what's happening." Arlene put it a different way. "I was laying there and all my glory, and people kept opening the door, looking in," she said. Don Murdoch, who would eventually go on to score the game-winning goal, never found out what was going on until recently. "I didn't know that, that's for sure," Murdoch said.

It must've seemed like an eternity for Arlene but not for her husband. "So, you know, it was basically over quicker than you can imagine," he said. "I remember very vividly that they said they asked if there was a hospital that I wanted them to take her to. My brother at that time was a staff physician at Beth Israel Hospital, so I suggested that they take us there."

As the ambulance they were riding in began to pull away from the Garden, there was a knock on the door and a photographer entered and took a picture. "I couldn't imagine why would anybody would be interested in this except us," Dr. Grossman said. "I guess I was wrong because when I arrived home from the hospital, I guess it was around 2:30 or three in the morning and I came into the house and the phone, my phone rang and it was Dick Young, who was the sports editor of the Daily News."

Young asked Dr. Grossman some questions about the birth, about his love for the Rangers and one that got him into some hot water with Arlene. "He asked me how old my wife was and the next day in the Daily News, on the front page of the newspaper, that a picture of the baby that was taken at the hospital and they had year, date of birth, not the date of birth but how old she was and here it was front page of the Daily News. So she's never forgiven me for that."

For 40 years, the Grossmans have answered inquiries as to why they didn't name their baby after a Rangers player or maybe even for the place where she was born. Arlene explained, "They said how come you didn't name her Madison? But my religion is that we name our children after a family member. Leah was Martin's mother's Hebrew name and Sloan was my father's name. So I never wanted to change what we had picked out to start with."

Leah did not inherit her parents' love for the Rangers as they moved to Florida when she was a young girl. Dr. Grossman said, "She was eight years old when we moved to Florida and she went to college here and became a Gators fan. She never, ever, really had what you would call an affinity for hockey."

The Grossman family has been amazed at the level of interest that has grown over the years by having their child born at Madison Square Garden and they've also embraced it. If you visit them at their Florida home, you will find the actual two seats from Section 336 that Dr. Grossman and Arlene sat in for the first period of Game 2 of the 1978 preliminary round against the Sabres, as well as a frame with Arlene's unused ticket hanging over it.

In a touch of irony, it was another Grossman child, who was not born at the Garden, who would have an impact on Rangers history. Leah's brother, Jay, has represented some of the highest profile NHL players as the president of PuckAgency. Two of his former clients were key members of the 1994 Stanley Cup-winning team, Hall of Famer Brian Leetch and fellow defenseman Sergei Zubov.

The game began with a sellout crowd, but, by the second period, grew by one. Sudden death, sudden birth. For Dr. Martin

Grossman and his wife, Arlene, it was the most memorable and eventful night they ever spent at Madison Square Garden.

Actual seats and unused ticket has a special place in the Grossman home.
(Photos courtesy of the Grossman Family)

CHAPTER 3
"THE FRANK SINATRA SONG"

The Rangers were the highest paid team in the league in 1978 but they were not getting much bang for their buck so Madison Square Garden president Sonny Werblin went to work.

Back when he was in charge of the American Football League's New York Jets in 1965, Werblin stunned the established National Football League by signing highly touted University of Alabama quarterback Joe Namath to the largest contract in pro football history. The sports entrepreneur would take the same approach to running the New York Rangers and it began with a bold signing somewhat similar to the Namath deal in that Werblin took on a competing league.

A pair of Swedish hockey players was thriving for the Winnipeg Jets in the rival World Hockey Association and word was out that they would become available to sign after the 1977–78 season.

For the previous four seasons, center Ulf Nilsson and right wing Anders Hedberg played alongside Hall of Famer Bobby Hull (who scored his 1000th career goal while playing with the duo) and they were putting up eye-opening numbers as part of the WHA's highest scoring line. Over that four-year period, Nilsson had 484 points in 300 career games including a league-leading 89 assists in 1977–78. Most of those assists were on goals scored by Hedberg, who found the back of the net 236 times (including a league-leading 70 during the 1976–77 season) in 286 career games.

The duo also led Winnipeg to two Avco Cup (the WHA version of the Stanley Cup) championships and three appearances in the finals.

The Rangers needed some new stars and an opportunity presented itself, so they began their pursuit of the Swedish superstars during the 1977–78 season. General manager John Ferguson would be instrumental in acquiring the services of the two stars, but he would not be around when they took the ice for the Rangers in 1978–79.

According to Nilsson, his and Hedberg's contracts had a clause where they could entertain offers from National Hockey League teams, but the Jets would be able to match. "If they [the Jets] matched the contract, we had to stay in Winnipeg," Nilsson said.

In February 1978, Ferguson invited Nilsson and Hedberg to a Rangers game at Madison Square Garden for a meeting with Garden brass. "Anders and I were invited down to New York when we played the Hartford [New England] Whalers," Nilsson said, "so we went down and had dinner with [Garden president] Sonny Werblin and [team president] Jack Krumpe in Suite 200." It turned out to be an amicable and productive meeting. Nilsson said Ferguson sold Werblin and Krumpe by not just highlighting their on-ice talents. "Ferguson said 'Well, these are really good guys' and Sonny Werblin said 'I really liked them as individuals.'" The feeling was mutual. "We liked what they [the Rangers] were trying to accomplish," Nilsson said. "If we came there, we would have a chance to win the Cup, that was our goal."

Hedberg admitted there were two reasons that he wanted to come to New York. "First of all, I think it was more money than the others, but then the other was the Frank Sinatra song ("New York, New York")." Hedberg felt if they could make it there, they could make it anywhere.

In late March, while he was broadcasting a nationally televised game between the New York Islanders and the Philadelphia Flyers (who were, ironically, being coached by Fred Shero), Ferguson announced the two stars would join the Rangers the following season. Nilsson and Hedberg originally agreed to two-year contracts, worth $475,000 per season, but Werblin felt that number wouldn't get the deal done. As many as five other teams were showing interest in the dynamic duo so Werblin wanted to one-up the competition, including the WHA Jets. "When he [Werblin] heard about that clause, he said 'We'll pay them $600,000 a year because we're not gonna give Winnipeg a chance to match it,'" Nilsson said.

In early June, the Rangers staged a lavish press conference to introduce their newest stars. Werblin reportedly spent $10,000 to put down an ice surface at the dormant Garden so the duo could show off their skating skills.

The Swedish stars knew they would be under a lot of pressure to help the Rangers end their Stanley Cup drought which stood at 38 years heading into the 1978–79 season. "We came to North America for the challenge of playing against the best," Hedberg said. "The NHL is the place for that and the biggest challenge is in New York."

They were also caught off guard as the Rangers hired a new general manager, who wasn't the person who brought them to New York, and a new coach. Four days earlier, the Rangers had fired Ferguson and coach Jean Guy Talbot and replaced them with Fred Shero, who assumed both roles. Nilsson sounded disappointed when he heard the news. "He [Ferguson] brought us here and we really liked Fergy but I guess that's part of the business," he said.

Hedberg admitted there was some initial trepidation because they had already met Ferguson and didn't know what to expect from Shero. "Freddy was very much different than John Ferguson but at the same time it was a warmth and understanding from Freddie," Hedberg said. "From that point, I said this will work out just fine."

There was also the issue of acceptance. European players had an unwarranted stigma attached to them that they didn't work hard so the North American players did not exactly welcome them with open arms. Hedberg said they had already faced that kind of discrimination. "In Winnipeg, we had gone through everything that you could go through in terms of being discriminated at the time Europeans were being discriminated," he said.

Both players made an effort to fit in by speaking English whenever they were with a third party. According to Hedberg, "Ulf and I had been over here for four years and in terms of language we used, we spoke English. If there was a third person around us, we switched to English immediately. We were very disciplined in that respect. I spoke Swedish if it was him and I alone somewhere in our room. Otherwise, it was English." The talented duo didn't abandon their native language, they were just trying to be respectful to their surroundings.

There would be no problem with Nilsson and Hedberg fitting right in with the Rangers. "The reason the Rangers got good is those two guys were the high compete," defenseman Mario Marois said. "They never backed down from anybody."

Rangers' defenseman Andre Dore felt the Swedish duo's humility helped them earn instant respect. "They didn't carry themselves with an air of entitlement. They came and they acted like they wanted to be good teammates right away," he said.

From the first practice, the Rangers knew they had something special. "They were kind of natural leaders," defenseman Mike McEwen said. "They were both kind of small, but they both played a big man's game. They weren't scared or nothing, they were just really good."

With the Swedes in place, Werblin's next task was to hire a general manager and coach. He was able to fill both holes with a single hire.

A Frank Sinatra song was a major reason that Anders Hedberg became a New York Ranger.
(Photo courtesy of Joanna Ente)

CHAPTER 4
THE FOG LIFTS THE RANGERS

Acquiring Ulf Nilsson and Anders Hedberg was Garden president Sonny Werblin's first major move and now he wanted to make a splash with the management team. Werblin saw a chance to acquire a big-name coach and a proven winner and he wasn't going to let that opportunity slip away.

It became well known that Werblin was looking to replace both John Ferguson and Jean Guy Talbot. There were reports that Flyers coach Fred Shero wanted to leave Philadelphia and had shown interest in becoming a general manager.

Three days after Shero, 52, resigned from Philadelphia, Werblin made contact with Mark Stewart, Shero's agent, to inquire if his client was available. Shero still had a year remaining on his contract with the Flyers but Werblin felt that the letter of resignation made him a free agent who would be eligible to sign with the Rangers.

Despite the Flyers' refusal to accept his resignation, Shero signed a five-year, $1.25 million-dollar deal to become the coach and general manager of the Rangers. In order to avoid tampering charges, Werblin agreed to send the Rangers' first-round pick in the 1978 NHL Draft to Philadelphia as compensation for Shero. (Philadelphia used the pick to select center Ken Linseman, who would play a role when the Rangers met the Flyers in the 1979 Stanley Cup quarterfinals and would go on to become one of the all-time Garden villains.)

On June 2, 1978, Fred "The Fog" Shero was introduced at the Hall of Fame Lounge at Madison Square Garden. There was some doubt as to whether he could handle both duties but Shero answered his critics by bluntly stating, "I know I can." Shero earned his nickname while playing for the St. Paul Saints of the United States Hockey League in 1948. One night, the high humidity in St. Paul created a fog on the ice that was so thick that none of the players could see. Shero claimed he could see the puck despite the poor visibility, thus he earned the nickname "Freddie the Fog."

Before Shero arrived, the Rangers were considered soft team lacking toughness, so the new coach wanted to change the culture. With Philadelphia, Shero had tough guys on the roster such as Dave Schultz and Ed Van Impe, players who epitomized the "Broad Street Bullies" philosophy that the Flyers employed to intimidate and push around their opponents, contributing to back-to-back Stanley Cup championships in 1974 and 1975.

The Rangers roster that Shero inherited did not have any of his preferred physical type players so he planned on making a few additions. "What you need on this team is the 'Van Impe' type," he said. "Mean, not tough, mean," Shero said. When informed that he did not have a physical type player on the roster, Shero defiantly responded, "Then we'll acquire one, but he has to be able to play in the league or he's not going to be any use to you."

The players did not know what to expect when Shero began his first training camp as the man in charge of the Rangers.

Defenseman Dave Maloney, who would later be named Shero's first captain, said the differences were immediately felt when the team moved its training camp from Long Beach, Long

Island to Westchester County. "We moved to Westchester," said Maloney. "There was just a new identity, everything changed."

Maloney remembered a small detail that the team worked on early in camp and it gave him a hint as to the type of hockey mind that would be coaching the team. "I do remember at one point, he had us defending with our sticks turned over," Maloney said. "So he was certainly more cerebral than Fergy and Jean-Guy [Talbot] were."

Center Walt Tkaczuk said Shero got his message across without actually speaking to anyone. "I wasn't sure what to think of him as he would come into the dressing room and write some things on the blackboard and then walk out or you'd walk into the dressing room and you'll see a certain saying he'd put on it and then you knew it was Fred put that up on the blackboard."

Left wing Pat Hickey said Shero would question players on the bench to see if they were paying attention to what's happening on the ice. "Freddie knew the answers to the questions he asked," Hickey said. "One game it was penalty filled (there were no coincidental penalties at the time) and he's runnin' up the bench and he's sorta playin' like he's in a fog. 'What's the situation here, what's the situation here, Maloney got a penalty and then [Ron] Duguay got a penalty.' I just turned around and told him what it was. 'Fred, we're a man short for 30 seconds and then we're gonna be even and then we're going to be a power play for 45 seconds. 'Okay, Hickey get out there.' That's the way that we got ice time."

Everything was new for Ulf Nilsson who was playing in the National Hockey League for the first time with one of the league's flagship franchises, along with a new coach. Nilsson said Shero helped him relax a bit in one of their early meetings. "He was sort of laid back, low key and things like that," Nilsson said, "but he said to me I'm never gonna play you after Phil Esposito. I realized why that was the case because Phil had a tendency to take ice time for two centermen."

Six weeks after he was hired, Shero and the Rangers took a punch to the gut. As a result of Don Murdoch's arrest for cocaine possession, NHL president John Ziegler suspended the 21-year-old winger for the entire 1978–79 season. Ziegler stipulated that the suspension would be commuted to 40 games upon an application for reinstatement by the Rangers. A request that would have to be made between the team's 30th and 35th regular season game.

Murdoch recently admitted he still has problems dealing with that episode of his life. "There's not a day that goes by when it's just, would've or could've," Murdoch said. "It was something in my life that's haunted me my whole life."

Murdoch was hoping to make an early impression on Shero, who didn't know the young winger, yet still supported him through this troubling time. "When I got the suspension, Fred Shero had me come in and I talked to him," said Murdoch. "He just said that, 'You know, you're a part of this team and we're gonna want you back.'"

Defenseman Mike McEwen was impressed with the way Shero ran practice. "His practices were some of the best practices that I've ever been involved in," he said. "He knew how to run a practice and drills were great and they really prepared you for a game."

Shero's reputation as a winner preceded him and that helped with the transition to coaching players who were already established. Left wing Steve Vickers was one of those players who welcomed the new coach. "I expected good things because Freddie Shero, he'd won in every league he'd coached in. He had the credentials to make us a good team."

Shero was a coach who delegated authority and responsibility, so he brought someone along from the Flyers who is considered one of the first prominent assistant coaches in NHL history. Mike Nykoluk was behind the bench as Shero's assistant when the Flyers won back-to-back Stanley Cups in 1974 and 1975 so his old boss decided to bring him to New York.

Nykoluk doesn't get enough credit for what he brought to the 1978–79 Rangers but the players did not dismiss his contribution. Nykoluk was a star with the Hershey Bears of the AHL for 14 seasons. McEwen said Nykoluk commanded instant respect. "He had a good eye for what was going on," McEwen said. "He was an extension of Freddie."

Right wing Lucien DeBlois said Shero had to juggle being both general manager and coach so he leaned on Nykoluk to handle some of the coach's other responsibilities. "Fred was the older GM so he had a lot of hats," DeBlois said. "Mike was the guy that worked day in and day out, especially me as a young guy doing some extra hours or whatever and talking to him, he was a tremendous personality."

Tkaczuk said Shero was very comfortable with handing off responsibilities to Nykoluk. "Fred never got on the ice very often in practice and Mike ran the practices. I felt that Mike was the person that should probably got more credit than he does."

Right before the season began, Shero would have to deal with naming a new team captain.

The Fog Lost two Finals as a Ranger—once as a player and once as head coach.
(Public domain photo via Wikimedia Commons)

CHAPTER 5
THE YOUNGEST CAPTAIN

Eighteen-year-old defenseman Dave Maloney became the youngest Ranger to play in a game when he made his NHL debut on December 18, 1974. Four years later, Fred Shero tabbed Maloney to be the youngest captain in team history.

On October 11, 1978, one day before the season began, Phil Esposito stepped down as team captain. Esposito reportedly felt the role was becoming a burden to him. Shero had seen enough in the 22-year-old defenseman, so he decided Maloney would be the player to wear the coveted "C" on the Ranger sweater as the 17th captain in team history.

Maloney said Shero broke the news to him away from the rink. "We had a sponsor's luncheon at the Rye Town Hilton and he pulled me aside after the luncheon and said 'You're going to be our next captain.'" Maloney admitted the decision caught him by surprise and not because he and the coach would never really speak much after that day. "That might've been about ten less words than the fifty I probably spoke to him as captain," he said.

Maloney was part of the Rangers' young core that featured a number of players who were under 25 years old, but the 36-year-old Esposito made a recommendation that would help shape the identity of the 1978–79 New York Rangers. "Phil had suggested that I was the guy," Maloney said, "because we were such a young group. I remember reading or hearing that he [Shero] saw some Bob Clarke (Shero's former player and Hall of Famer with the

Philadelphia Flyers) in me."

There was a consensus among the players that Maloney displayed a burning desire to win. "To me, why play if you can't win?" Maloney said. Shero felt Maloney had the right makeup to be the kind of leader that he was looking for. "Whatever that was, that compete, or the willingness to kind of step out on a limb and maybe stand up and speak or do what you had to do," Maloney said. The 22-year-old embraced the new responsibilities. "I wasn't afraid of being a guy that had to be or whatever the circumstance called for," he said.

Pat Hickey recalled that he and several veteran players including Phil Esposito, Carol Vadnais, Steve Vickers, and John Davidson met formally with Shero at a local restaurant to discuss the captaincy. "That was the captain, that was the leadership appointing David and we all agreed, and my recollection is, it didn't really matter. We were all rooting for each other anyway and he [Shero] put together that committee."

Hickey said Shero pulled him aside to ask for some advice concerning Maloney. "The purpose of that was, he was concerned if the young guys, the Farrishes, and McEwens, and Murdochs, and Maroises, could relate to Phil and Vad [Vadnais] because they are pretty dominant personalities," he said.

According to Hickey, Shero felt the younger players would relate better to a younger team captain. "Vickers, J.D., and myself were in the middle and it was easier for us to tell Phil where to go than it is for Mike McEwen to tell Phil where to go," Hickey said, "and that's the way he explained it to me. As it turned out, Phil was more cool with the young guys."

With a team that still featured veteran players such as Esposito, Vadnais, Walt Tkaczuk and Vickers, Maloney was not going to be intimidated by wearing the "C" for this proud franchise. "It was always a respected position within the room," Maloney said. "You were expected to be the guy, that kind of be the go-between, and things like that, but I never looked at it. I was never intimidated by it and maybe I should've been."

Vickers felt a single letter on the sweater did not designate leadership. "The captain thing is overrated," Vickers said. "I think you lead on the ice."

The role was difficult because a captain had to be concerned about his own game while balancing the team's needs and performing the off-ice duties that go along with the territory. "I wasn't hesitant to speak," said Maloney, "most times I got along pretty well with the media." To the point where some of his teammates gave him some good-natured ribbing. "Gresch [Ron Greschner] said he [Maloney] never kept his mouth shut."

It didn't take long for Maloney to earn the respect in the room. Goaltender John Davidson said the move wasn't met with any resistance. "No, I honestly don't remember anybody complaining about it. With older people around, such as Espo, etc., everybody had a way of providing leadership."

Mario Marois said Esposito still led, even though he wasn't the captain anymore, and that was a big help to Maloney. "It started with an older guy [Esposito] who's still supporting Dave," Marois said. "I would think Carol Vadnais had a part in this too to support the captain at the time."

At the time Maloney was named captain, Ulf Nilsson was just trying to fit in, but he recognized the leadership skills in the 22-year-old. "He was a hardworking guy, very intense. Wanted to win so badly," he said.

Defenseman Dave Farrish said Shero was ahead of his time by naming a young player to be team captain. "It's one of those deals where you see a lot of current NHL teams with younger captains and Fred was probably one of the first guys to ever do that. So it was just another way he was so much ahead of his time with the hockey world and everything else."

Making what was an outside the box decision in those days was typical of Shero's ability to reach players using unique methods of motivation. "Obviously, it was a signal to the young guys because there was a really good crop of those, three years in a row of very good draft choices, that were going to become a big part of the core," Farrish said. "I think he just thought, you know, we'll give it to a younger guy that's going to be around for a lotta years instead of another, maybe another older player that might only play one more, whatever. So you'd have to get inside his head which is not easy to do, and figuring out why he did it. Obviously, in retrospect, it was a good move."

Farrish and Maloney had been teammates for two seasons before the 1978–79 season began. "Dave was very serious about his hockey," Farrish said. "He was a very serious individual about all the stuff, not only hockey but his lifestyle, the whole deal. You know, he was a very mature 22-year-old and I think that obviously played into the way he competed. All the parts of his game, his personality. I think all led in that direction. I think that's what Fred recognized."

Fred Shero made Dave Maloney the youngest captain in Rangers history..
(Photo courtesy of Joanna Ente)

CHAPTER 6
OCTOBER: FAST START

With a Stanley Cup–winning coach behind the bench, a pair of highly touted International stars, and a core of young talent, there was an air of anticipation surrounding the Rangers as the 1978–79 season opener approached.

According to goaltender John Davidson, the playoff loss to Buffalo the previous season prepared the Rangers for what was to come. "It's something that eats at you, but the next time around, when you get into the playoffs, you know what the world's about. It's a different world for a number of different reasons. You know, expectations. How good your team is, how good the other team is, and how to win at all costs. It's just different. It's hard and it's great, but the experience is so important."

Game 1, Thursday, October 12, 1978
Rangers 3 vs. Philadelphia Flyers 3 @ MSG (0–0–1)

The opening game of the 1978–79 season had a touch of irony as Fred Shero made his Rangers coaching debut at Madison Square Garden against his old team, the Philadelphia Flyers. There was much anticipation for this opener because of a bench-clearing brawl between the teams in a preseason game at the Garden (see Chapter 13).

Before a raucous Garden crowd, the Rangers scored three

power play goals to take a 3–0 lead. Steve Vickers, Pat Hickey and Mike McEwen each scored with the man advantage to give the home team a 3–0 lead after one period. The Flyers stormed back with two goals in the second before Paul Holmgren scored on a power play to tie the game with 1:12 remaining.

The teams settled for a point, but Philadelphia extended their unbeaten streak against the Rangers to 13 in a row.

Game 2, Sunday, October 15, 1978
Rangers 4 vs. Colorado Rockies 1 @ MSG (1–0–1)

There was a bit of uncertainty at Madison Square Garden going into the third period of the second game of the season. The Rangers were looking for their first win under new coach Fred Shero but they were locked in a 1–1 tie with the Colorado Rockies.

That trepidation intensified as the period went on but with a little over four minutes remaining, the Rangers took a 2–1 lead on center Ron Duguay's first goal of the season. Mike McEwen, who scored the Rangers' first goal, his second of the season, began the winning play with a dump in along the right-wing boards. Right wing Pierre Plante played the puck toward the Rockies' net and Duguay was able to lift it past goaltender Doug Favell for the go-ahead goal.

Left wing Greg Polis scored his first of the season with less than two minutes left for a 3–1 lead. Anders Hedberg put the icing on the cake with his first NHL goal into an empty net with 13 seconds remaining.

Thanks to a stout defensive effort by the Rangers, goaltender John Davidson faced only one shot on goal in the third period and made 12 of 13 saves overall.

During a recent interview, Davidson reflected on his first season with the New York Rangers in 1975 when he faced the Flyers on back to back nights and faced a total of nearly 90 shots. In that season, the Rangers' had a porous defense leading to an inordinate amount of shots and goals against.

"After the second game at home, I showered after the game," Davidson recalled, "and went through the medical room and the doctor grabbed me and said, 'I want to see you tomorrow.' I said, 'Listen, Doc, I'm tired, I'm going home, I'm staying home.' He says, 'No, I wanna see you' I say, 'What for?' He said, 'Count the bruises,' and I didn't even realize it. There were something like 14 or 16 black and blue marks."

Davidson did not want to pay the doctor a visit, so he downplayed the marks on his body. "Well, this is what happens. This is hockey," he said. "He [the doctor] says, 'Well, I want to test your blood.' He says, 'It looks like you're bruising easily, you never know, it could be a leukemia thing, you've gotta get tested,' so I went and got tested but it was nothing, it was just hockey. It was a price of what we did and that's because of the work I had against the Flyers."

John Davidson " It was the price of what we did"
(Photo courtesy of New York Rangers)

Game 3, Wednesday, October 18, 1978
Rangers 3 vs. Detroit Red Wings 3 @MSG (1-0-2)

The Rangers came from behind to earn a point as right wing Dean Talafous's first goal as a Ranger tied the game in the third period against the Detroit Red Wings. Mike McEwen scored his third goal in three games. The tie completed a three-game homestand to open the season.

Game 4, Thursday, October 19, 1978
Rangers 2 @ Detroit Red Wings 2 (1–0–3)

The second of a home-and-home with the Red Wings produced the same result as the teams played to a 2–2 tie in the Rangers' first road game of the season. For the second straight game, the Rangers came from behind in the third period.

The Blueshirts trailed 2–0 late in the game when Walt Tkaczuk and Lucien DeBlois scored 55 seconds apart to beat Red Wings goaltender Jim Rutherford.

Game 5, Saturday, October 21, 1978
@ New York Islanders 5 Rangers 3 (1–1–3)

The Rangers' first visit to the Nassau Coliseum in 1978–79 was a disappointment as the Islanders defeated them, 5–3.

The Islanders jumped to a 4–0 lead before center Ulf Nilsson scored his first goal in a Ranger uniform in the third period. Phil Esposito and Mario Marois rounded out the scoring with their first goals of the season as the Rangers suffered their first loss.

Game 6, Sunday, October 22, 1978
Rangers 5 Maple Leafs 2 @ MSG (2–1–3)

The Rangers scored four goals in the third period to power past the Toronto Maple Leafs in a 5–2 win at the Garden.

With the game tied at one in the third period, Phil Esposito's second goal of the season snapped the tie. Ulf Nilsson, Dean Talafous, and Lucien DeBlois each scored their second goal of the season as the Rangers remained unbeaten at home.

A Monday skate that followed a Sunday night game was usually optional, but Pat Hickey said Fred Shero proved he was a master motivator when he addressed the team after the game. "Fred walks in after we won, 5–2, on Sunday night and he said, 'Okay, optional practice tomorrow, who wants to coach?' and with what my little relationship with Freddie was, I put my hand up right away, so he says, 'Hickey's runnin' practice,' and as he always did, walked out. Phil [Esposito] was the first one come over to me and he says, 'Can I run it, can I give you some drills, I wanna work on something' and I said, 'No, I'm running practice.' Fred pops his head back in and says, 'I think tomorrow's practice shouldn't be optional, I think it's mandatory. Everybody be there, Hickey's running it.' Obviously, it was contrived."

Hickey said even though he was the designated coach for the optional practice, other players had input into what was done during the session. "The next morning, we all showed up and everybody came with a recommendation, a wish list and that's what we did," Hickey said. "That became a little bit of a routine for the optional practices and kind of the theme of that year. I don't think anybody really missed an optional practice because it was just a lot of fun to go to."

Pat Hickey raised his hand to run an optional practice.
(Photo courtesy of Pat Hickey)

Game 7, Wednesday, October 25, 1978
Rangers 6 Vancouver Canucks 2 @ MSG (3–1–3)

The Rangers exploded for four goals within a 4:12 span of the second period en route to a 6–2 win over the Vancouver Canucks at Madison Square Garden.

Anders Hedberg got the barrage started with his second goal of the season to snap a scoreless tie. Defenseman Carol Vadnais scored his first, Steve Vickers added his second of the season, and Ulf Nilsson scored for the third straight game to give the Rangers a 4–0 lead after two periods.

In the third period, Lucien DeBlois and Dean Talafous added

their third goals of the season to round out the offensive outburst as the Rangers improved their home record to 3–0–2.

Game 8, Saturday, October 28, 1978
Rangers 2 @ Montreal Canadiens 1 (4–1–3)

Goaltender Wayne Thomas stopped 31 shots to beat his old team in a 2–1 victory over the defending Stanley Cup champion Montreal Canadiens at the Forum.

The Rangers led, 1-0, in the second period when Canadiens right wing Guy Lafleur, a future Hall of Famer, hit the post and nearly tied the game. "I saw it all the way," Thomas joked after the game.

Montreal tied the game in the third on a goal by Lafleur but Steve Vickers scored his third goal of the season midway through the final period to secure the Rangers' third straight win.

Game 9, Sunday, October 29, 1978
Rangers 3 Pittsburgh Penguins 2 @ MSG (5–1–3)

The Blueshirts closed the month of October with their fourth win in a row as they got past the Pittsburgh Penguins, 3–2, at Madison Square Garden.

The Rangers trailed, 1-0, in the second period when defenseman Ron Greschner scored on the power play. Less than four minutes later, Pat Hickey put the Rangers in front off a feed from Greschner. Pierre Plante's goal late in the second period proved to be enough as the Rangers snapped a five-game home losing streak to the Penguins, who they had not beaten at the Garden in nearly three years.

CHAPTER 7
NOVEMBER: BUILDING AN IDENTITY

The Rangers were coming off a successful first month of the regular season (5–1–3, 13 points) and were in second place, two points behind the unbeaten Atlanta Flames in the Patrick Division. The Rangers extended their road winning streak to seven games as the month came to an end.

Game 10, Thursday, November 2, 1978
Rangers 3 @ Colorado Rockies 0 (6–1–3)

The Rangers continued to roll as they took to the road and blanked the Colorado Rockies, 3–0, for their fifth consecutive win.

Wayne Thomas stopped 26 shots in posting the shutout. Steve Vickers and Dave Maloney scored goals in a less than a 90-second span of the first period as the Rangers improved to 2–1–1 away from Madison Square Garden.

Game 11, Saturday, November 4, 1978
Rangers 7 @ Los Angeles Kings 3 (7–1–3)

Ulf Nilsson scored twice and Dave Maloney added a short-handed goal as the Rangers walloped the Los Angeles Kings, 7–3.

Nilsson's first goal of the night tied the game, 2–2, late in the first period. It also began a streak of six unanswered goals to put the Rangers up by a 7–2 margin. The Swedish center scored his second of the game in the second period to snap the deadlock as the Rangers coasted to their sixth straight victory.

John Davidson was the beneficiary of the offensive output as he stopped 21 of 24 shots and beat the Kings for the first time in eight tries.

Game 12, Sunday, November 5, 1978
Rangers 5 @ Vancouver Canucks 2 (8–1–3)

Ron Duguay and Phil Esposito each had a goal and two assists while Ron Greschner, Dave Farrish, and Pat Hickey each added a goal and an assist in the Rangers' 5–2 win over the Canucks in Vancouver for their seventh straight win.

Wayne Thomas stopped 22 of 24 shots as the Rangers got off to their best start since the 1971–72 season when they lost only once in their first 17 games.

Game 13, Wednesday, November 8, 1978
Minnesota North Stars 5 Rangers 3 @MSG (8–2–3)

The Rangers had their seven-game winning streak snapped upon their return home from a successful three game Western swing.

Goaltender Gilles Meloche made 34 saves in keying the North Stars' 5–3 win, giving new head coach Glen Sonmor a win in his first game after replacing former Ranger Harry Howell after the team started the season 3–6–2. Minnesota led, 4–0, after two periods but goals from Ron Duguay, Ron Greschner, and Ulf Nilsson made the final score respectable.

Gilles Meloche stops Phil Esposito as well as the Rangers seven game win streak
(Photo courtesy of Joanna Ente)

Game 14, Saturday, November 11, 1978
Rangers 2 @ Pittsburgh Penguins 1 (9–2–3)

Doug Soetaert got the start in net and made 46 saves to lead the Rangers past the Penguins, 2-1, in Pittsburgh for their eighth win in their last nine games and fifth straight on the road.

Ron Duguay's sixth goal of the season gave the Rangers a 1–0 lead in the first period. Soetaert was particularly brilliant in the second period as he stopped 18 of 19 Penguins shots.

Phil Esposito stuffed one in past Penguins goalie Denis Herron early in the second for a 2–0 lead. Late in the second period Pittsburgh right wing Peter Lee scored a power play goal to break up the shutout bid.

Game 15, Sunday, November 12, 1978
New York Islanders 5 Rangers 3 @MSG (9–3–3)

The Islanders beat the Rangers for the second straight time as they scored a 5–3 win at Madison Square Garden.

Wayne Thomas had a rough night as he gave up five goals on 21 shots. The Islanders took a 1–0 lead in the first period when defenseman Stefan Persson blasted a 30-foot shot past Thomas. Ron Greschner's fifth goal of the season tied the game after one.

The Islanders took the lead for good in the second period. With the teams skating four-on-four, Islanders center Lorne Henning scored his first goal of the season for a 2–1 lead. Less than two minutes later, future Hall of Famer Clark Gillies tipped in Persson's shot from the point for a two-goal advantage.

Rangers right wing Eddie Johnstone narrowed the deficit with his first goal of the season, but Islanders center Bob Bourne scored less than a minute later to make it 4–2.

In the third period, Mike McEwen's fifth goal of the season cut the Isles' lead to 4–3 and had the Garden crowd in a frenzy. Future Hall of Famer Mike Bossy closed out the scoring with his eighth goal of the season as the Rangers lost for only the second time in their last ten games.

Game #16, Wednesday, November 15, 1978
Rangers 8 Chicago Black Hawks 1 @ MSG (10–3–3)

Pat Hickey scored his first National Hockey League hat trick (he had one playing for the Toronto Toros in the World Hockey Association) and combined with linemates Ulf Nilsson and Anders Hedberg for 13 points as the Rangers routed the Chicago Black Hawks, 8–1.

Hickey's hat trick and two assists accounted for a five-point night, while Nilsson also had a five-point night with a goal and four assists. Hedberg scored a goal and added two assists as the Rangers continued to pile up the points in winning for the ninth time in their last 11 games.

The Rangers ride Hitch's big night to a 8–1 win over Chicago.
(Photo courtesy of Pat Hickey)

Game 17, Saturday, November 18, 1978
Rangers 7 @ Minnesota North Stars 2 (11–3–3)

The Rangers got some payback for having their seven-game win streak snapped with a 7–2 victory.

The Blueshirts' hottest line made it easy for Wayne Thomas to pick up a win. Pat Hickey, Anders Hedberg, and Ulf Nilsson each scored a goal and combined for eight points while Carol Vadnais scored twice.

Game 18, Sunday, November 19, 1978
Atlanta Flames 3 Rangers 1 @ MSG (11–4–3)

The Rangers continued to have trouble winning against the Atlanta Flames as they lost, 3–1, at Madison Square Garden. It was the 14th time in 17 games that the Rangers could not beat the Flames.

Phil Esposito's eighth goal of the season gave the Rangers a 1–0 lead after the first period but Atlanta scored three unanswered goals to continue their domination of the home team.

Flames right wing Jean Pronovost beat John Davidson midway through the second period to tie the game at one. Center Guy Chouinard scored his 13th goal of the season for a 2–1 lead in the third. Left wing Eric Vail completed the scoring.

Defenseman Mike McEwen was a minus-2 on the night and had some costly giveaways. McEwen recalled that he was frustrated with himself that night and pointed to coach Fred Shero's ability to push the right buttons to settle him down.

"I was an offensive defenseman and a lot of times I tried to get offense started in my own end and it backfired," McEwen said. "That happened about four or five times a year, just give the puck away badly in our end. I did it once and this guy just [scores] a goal, it's like "boom-boom," what the fuck and I'm skating to the bench and I'm all pissed off and I get to the bench, and it's at the Garden and everybody is pissed off at me.

McEwen added that what Shero did next was exactly what he needed. "I sit down and I'm like, fuck, and I'm like pissed right. Then he comes up behind and puts his hand under my fuckin' jersey and starts rubbing my back. He says, 'It's okay. You know what you did wrong and you won't do it again,' and he's rubbing your back. Shit. At that moment, I'm thinking 'I'll go through a wall for this guy.'"

You know what you did wrong and you won't do it again."
(Photo courtesy of Joanna Ente)

Game 19, Wednesday, November 22, 1978
Rangers 3 Toronto Maple Leafs 3 @MSG (11-4-4)

In a back-and-forth contest, the Rangers and Toronto Maple Leafs finished in a 3–3 tie at Madison Square Garden in a game that featured a fight within the first minute of the game.

Just 13 seconds in, Maple Leafs enforcer Tiger Williams cross-checked Carol Vadnais into the boards and they dropped the gloves for a short encounter that observers would rule a draw. The confrontation set a tone for what proved to be a very physical encounter.

Leafs center Pat Boutette, another noted tough guy, mixed it up with Anders Hedberg while Toronto's Dan Maloney, who was widely regarded as the best pound-for-pound fighter in the National Hockey League, clutched and grabbed Pierre Plante.

The physical play came as no surprise to Fred Shero. "We expected a physical contest," said the coach. "I must say they came out hitting but we hit back too, and that made the difference."

The Rangers held a 3–2 lead in the third period but Toronto tied the game with 3:05 remaining when center Bruce Boudreau broke in alone and beat goaltender Doug Soetaert from ten feet out for his second goal of the game.

Rangers left wing Nick Fotiu had a couple of small skirmishes during the game but things broke loose when the final buzzer sounded. Looking to get even for the Leafs' physical play, Fotiu started a brawl with Williams. Shero admitted that they were looking for payback. "Yes, we sent Nicky in there. Not many guys want to tangle with him."

"Not many guys want to tangle with him"
(Photo by Mark Rosenman)

Game 20, Sunday November 26, 1978
Rangers 9 Washington Capitals 4 @ MSG (12-4-4)

Scoring nine goals on 30 shots against Caps goalie Jim Bedard, the Rangers blasted Washington, 9-4, at Madison Square Garden. Anders Hedberg and Ron Greschner each scored twice while Carol Vadnais had a big game with three assists.

Steve Vickers, Phil Esposito, and Greschner all scored in the first period to give the Rangers a 3–1 lead after one. Hedberg scored both of his goals in the second period when the Rangers scored four goals on eight shots.

Mike McEwen added his sixth goal of the season while Eddie Johnstone scored his second and Pat Hickey his ninth to round out the scoring with 33 seconds left in the game.

Game 21, Wednesday, November 29, 1978

Rangers 5 @ Atlanta Flames 3 (13–4–4)

In winning their seventh straight game on the road, the Rangers got off the schneid against their nemesis, the Atlanta Flames. They had dropped seven straight and 11 of 12 to Atlanta.

Dean Talafous scored two goals to snap a 1–1 tie in the second period. The Blueshirts took a 5–1 lead in the third period on goals by Lucien DeBlois and Pat Hickey before Atlanta scored two late goals.

After the game, coach Fred Shero said, "Atlanta wasn't being as physical with us as usual, but maybe we were just due to win." Before the game, he had called out some unnamed players for a lack of effort against the Flames. "I know who among us is not giving as good effort as they should against Atlanta, but I'm not naming names," Shero said about what he told the team before the game.

John Davidson made 33 saves and was relieved to have finally beaten the Flames. "We decided to just go out there and play without thinking about the pressure of ending the losing streak," he said.

CHAPTER 8
DECEMBER: GETTIN' BUSY

Following an 8–3–1 record in November, the Rangers fell to third place in the tightly contested Patrick Division with 30 points. They trailed the second-place Islanders by one point and they were only two behind the first-place Flames. December would prove to be a very busy month with 16 games on the schedule.

Game 22, Saturday, December 2, 1978
@ Toronto Maple Leafs 5 Rangers 2 (13–5–4)

The Rangers took a 2–0 lead in the second period but the Toronto Maple Leafs scored five unanswered goals for a 5–2 victory at Maple Leaf Gardens. The loss snapped the Blueshirts' seven-game road winning streak.

Goals by Anders Hedberg and Lucien DeBlois gave the Rangers a two-goal lead before future Hall of Famer Darryl Sittler scored twice within a two-minute span to tie the game. Pat Boutette added two goals and continued to mix it up with Hedberg, which he did in the teams' previous meeting in New York. Ron Duguay also fought former Ranger right wing Jerry Butler.

Game 23, Sunday, December 3, 1978
Boston Bruins 3 Rangers 2 @ MSG (13–6–4)

The Rangers rallied from a 2–0 deficit but couldn't hold off the Boston Bruins who won their eighth consecutive game at Madison Square Garden with a 3–2 win.

Bruins defenseman Al Sims blasted a 55-foot shot past John Davidson at 1:03 of the second period to give Boston a 2–0 lead.

Phil Esposito's 10th goal of the season cut the deficit to one. In the third period, Ulf Nilsson scored a short-handed, breakaway goal to tie the game, but Bruins left wing John Wensink scored with less than four minutes left to give Boston their eighth win in a row on Eighth Avenue. The Rangers hadn't beaten the Bruins at home since March 23, 1975.

Game 24, Wednesday, December 6, 1978
Rangers 7 St. Louis Blues 4 @ MSG (14–6–4)

Phil Esposito scored two goals and Steve Vickers added a goal and two assists as the Rangers ended a two-game losing streak with a 7–4 win over the St. Louis Blues at Madison Square Garden. Just as Boston dominated the Rangers on Garden ice, the Broadway Blueshirts have dominated the Blues at home since their inception in 1967. In their first 30 matchups at the Garden, the Rangers defeated the Blues 26 times, losing only once, with three ties. The only St. Louis win at MSG came in November 1968.

Espo scored both of his goals in the first period. Ron Duguay, Anders Hedberg, Pat Hickey, and Walt Tkaczuk also scored. Carol Vadnais, Lucien DeBlois, and Mike McEwen had two assists each.

Esposito's two goals keyed the win over St. Louis.
(Photo courtesy of Joanna Ente)

Game 25, Thursday, December 7, 1978
Rangers 5 @ Philadelphia Flyers 2 (15–6–4)

Rallying from a 2-0 deficit with five unanswered goals, the Rangers beat the Philadelphia Flyers for the first time since April 1975 and it was also their first win at the Spectrum since February 1974.

Ron Greschner scored a power play goal to snap a 2–2 tie in the third period and Walt Tkaczuk added a goal 30 seconds later as the Rangers won both games of a back-to-back portion of the schedule.

Pat Hickey and Carol Vadnais had drawn the Blueshirts even

with second-period goals in just over a two-minute span. Ulf Nilsson added an empty netter for his 10th goal of the season.

Walt Tkaczuk scored an insurance goal 30 seconds after Ron Greschner gave the Rangers the lead against the Flyers.
(Photo courtesy of New York Rangers / NHL [Public domain] via Wikimedia Commons)

Game 26, Saturday, December 9, 1978
@Detroit Red Wings 5 Rangers 4 (15–7–4)

The Rangers blew a 3–0 lead and suffered their worst loss of the season as they were beaten by the Red Wings in Detroit, 5–4.

Red Wings left wing Dan Bolduc scored the first two goals of his NHL career in the third period to key the win. Bolduc's first tally gave Detroit a 4–3 lead at 42 seconds into the third period but Walt Tkaczuk tied the game for the Rangers with less than 10 minutes left. Bolduc beat John Davidson at 16:46 of the third period to hand the Rangers a bitter defeat.

Game 27, Sunday, December 10, 1978
Philadelphia Flyers 4 Rangers 0 @MSG (15–8–4)

A wild night at Madison Square Garden saw the Rangers shut out by goaltender Bernie Parent and the Philadelphia Flyers, 4–0.

The "Broad Street Bullies" were out in force and the Garden crowd went right along with the program as they were chanting obscenities and tossed items like toilet paper on the ice that delayed the game along the way.

Things got real ugly in the second period when Flyers right wing Paul Holmgren swung his stick and chopped down on the helmet of Carol Vadnais in retaliation after the Ranger defenseman had speared him.

After coach Fred Shero walked onto the ice to check on his player, referee Bob Myers levied a bench penalty on the Rangers. "I thought my player was dead, don't I have a right to find out?" Shero wanted to know. Holmgren was ejected but the Rangers were short-handed.

In all, 22 penalties were called. The Rangers had four power plays, including a 5-on-3 at one point, and couldn't put the puck past Parent, who made 28 saves.

Game 28, Wednesday, December 13, 1978
Rangers 8 Los Angeles Kings 7 @ MSG (16–8–4)

In a game that featured six ties and seven lead changes, the Rangers outscored the Kings, 8–7, at Madison Square Garden.

The teams were tied at three after one period of play. LA's Butch Goring opened the scoring with a goal at 4:09 of the first period but Pierre Plante tied the game just 42 seconds later. Phil Esposito's 13th goal of the season gave the Rangers their first lead of the game. The Kings scored the next two goals before Steve Vickers made it 3–3.

In the second period, the Rangers took a 4–3 lead on Lucien DeBlois's goal but the Kings regained the lead by scoring the next two goals. Ron Greschner scored his 10th goal to tie the game, 5–5, but former Ranger Mike Murphy put the Kings ahead with 34 seconds left in the second period.

Vickers's second goal of the game, his ninth of the season, early in the third tied the game at six. Greschner's second goal of the night gave the Rangers a 7–6 lead and Ulf Nilsson scored the Rangers' eighth goal less than 90 seconds later before the Kings made it close. Wayne Thomas replaced John Davidson in goal at the start of the third period and earned the win.

Game 29, Saturday, December 16, 1978
@ Boston Bruins 4 Rangers 1 (16–9–4)

The Rangers lost for the fifth time in their last eight games, dropping a 4–1 decision to the Bruins at Boston Garden.

Phil Esposito scored the Rangers' lone goal, his 14th, and after the game lamented the team's lethargic play of late. "We play so well, then we play absolutely rotten and it drives me nuts."

His goal narrowed Boston's lead to 2–1 late in the second period, but the goal that burned the Rangers came a little over a minute later as the result of a mistake. Boston's John Wensink got behind Mario Marois and broke in alone to beat Wayne Thomas for a 3–1 lead.

The loss was their fourth straight against the Bruins, dating back to last season. In their last 15 meetings, the Rangers have beaten Boston only once with one tie.

Following the loss, Esposito called out himself and his teammates. "Every once in a while, the guys on this team, including myself, think we're All-Stars." he said. "We've got to learn that when we all work together as a team, we win. It's that simple."

During the practice session that followed this dismal loss, Dean Talafous related a story about Fred Shero that told a lot about why he was able to get players to play hard for him.

Talafous was not in the everyday lineup and did not dress for the game in Boston. Before practice began, Talafous said Shero was on the bench and yelled for him to come over. "I went over and I sat next to him while everybody was kind of loosening up," Talafous said recently. "He says, 'Why do you think we lost last night?' and I can remember I said 'I don't want to, you know, I don't want to talk bad about my teammates obviously,' but I said, 'I think that particular night Boston wanted it more than us.'"

To this day, Shero's response had a great impact on Talafous and the rest of the Rangers. "He says, 'As long as I'm general manager and coach the New York Rangers, you'll never sit out another game,' and I never did," Talafous said. "He put his trust in you and because of that, I went through the glass for him the whole time I was up there because he believed in me and he made a promise and kept it."

Game 30, Sunday, December 17, 1978
Boston Bruins 4 Rangers 1 @ MSG (16-10-4)

Former Ranger Rick Middleton scored twice as the Bruins completed a sweep of the home-and-home series with a second consecutive 4–1 win. The Bruins won their fifth in a row over the Rangers and it was their ninth straight win at the Garden.

After a scoreless first period, Middleton scored his first goal at 6:50 of the second period. The assists went to former Rangers Brad Park and Jean Ratelle. Pat Hickey tied the game with his 14th goal but the Bruins took the lead for good on a goal by center Mike Walton midway through the second period.

The Bruins' grinding and hardworking style was on full display as they continued to dominate their ex-teammate Phil Esposito and the Rangers. After the game, Esposito was asked why the Bruins always seemed to play so hard every game. Espo replied, "Because Boston is such a great place to play, you work your tail off to stay there."

Game 31, Wednesday, December 20, 1978
Rangers 6 Buffalo Sabres 3 @ MSG (17–10–4)

Dean Talafous scored twice to snap a personal nine-game scoreless streak in leading the Rangers to a 6–3 win over the Buffalo Sabres at Madison Square Garden. The victory snapped a two-game losing streak.

Talafous's first goal of the night gave the Rangers a 2–1 lead early in the second period. Phil Esposito scored his 15th goal later in the period for a 3–1 lead.

The Rangers put the game away with three goals in the third period. Talafous scored his second of the game and ninth of the season while Mario Marois and Anders Hedberg found the back of the net before the Sabres scored a late consolation goal.

Dean Talafous (left) chipped in to break a two-game losing streak.
(Photo courtesy of Joanna Ente)

Game 32, Friday, December 22, 1978
Rangers 4 Detroit Red Wings 2 @ MSG (18–10–4)

Phil Esposito and Pat Hickey each scored twice to lead the Rangers to a 4–2 win over the Detroit Red Wings at Madison Square Garden. Espo's first goal of the game snapped a 2–2 tie with five seconds left in the first period and it proved to be the game-winner.

Hickey scored both of his goals in the first period which ended with the Rangers leading, 3–2. Esposito completed the scoring with an empty-net goal late in the third period.

Game 33, Saturday, December 23, 1978
@ New York Islanders 9 Rangers 4 (18–11–4)

Heading into this latest edition of the rivalry, the Rangers, who were in last place, trailed the New York Islanders by seven points for the top spot in the Patrick Division, so they were hoping to have a big night and make a statement in the process.

Islanders' center Bryan Trottier scored five goals to lead a 9–4 rout of the Rangers at Nassau Coliseum. The Rangers continued to have trouble winning on Long Island as they lost for seventh time in their last eight games there with one tie.

Trottier got the scoring started in the first period with his 20th goal of the season. Ron Greschner tied the game with his 12th and the teams were tied, 1–1, after one.

The home team blew the game open by scoring seven times in the second period. Mike Bossy gave the Islanders a 2–1 lead with a power play goal and then Trottier made it 3–1 with his second of the game.

The Islanders poured it on against Wayne Thomas, who was replaced by John Davidson after two periods after Trottier's third goal made it 8–2.

Trottier scored his fourth and fifth in the third period, receiving credit for the Islanders' ninth goal, which was originally credited to Stefan Persson.

It was an embarrassing night for the Rangers, but it added fuel to the fire for what was yet to come.

Game 34, Tuesday, December 26, 1978
Rangers 5 @ Atlanta Flames 3 (19–11–4)

The Rangers rallied from a two-goal deficit to stun the Flames with a 5–3 win in Atlanta.

After Atlanta's Bill Clement scored in the opening minute of the second period, the Rangers trailed, 3–1, but then they broke through for four unanswered goals. Anders Hedberg and Nick Fotiu scored 15 seconds apart to tie the game. Later in the period, Mike McEwen scored his 10th goal while Pierre Plante capped off an impressive offensive display.

John Davidson was the beneficiary of the Rangers' domination as they outshot the Flames, 43–23.

Game 35, Thursday, December 28, 1978
@ Philadelphia Flyers 6 Rangers 5 (19–12–4)

The Rangers could never seem to get over the hump against the Flyers in a 6–5 loss to their hated rivals at the Spectrum.

Despite being outshot, 20–8, after two periods, the Rangers were tied with the Flyers, 3–3, scoring two second-period goals on four shots as Ulf Nilsson scored his 12th and Ron Greschner his 14th.

Bobby Clarke scored less than a minute into the third period to give Philly a 4–3 lead but Phil Esposito beat Flyers goalie Bernie Parent to tie the game. After Reggie Leach scored to give the Flyers a 5–4 lead, Steve Vickers tied the game once more with a power play goal, his 10th of the season.

With 3:22 remaining, Philadelphia's Paul Holmgren skated around the net and stuffed a wraparound past goaltender Doug

Soetaert for the game-winner.

Game 36, Saturday, December 30, 1978
Rangers 5 @ Chicago Black Hawks 4 (20–12–4)

The Rangers took a 3–0 lead and never looked back as they beat the Black Hawks in Chicago, 5–4.

Goals by Anders Hedberg, Ron Duguay, and Ulf Nilsson put the Rangers up by three in the first period. After Chicago cut the lead to 3–2 in the second period, Pat Hickey scored on the power play and Hedberg's second goal of the game helped restore the Rangers' three-goal cushion.

Chicago made it a one–goal game late in the third, but the Rangers held on for their 20th win of the season.

Game 37, Sunday, December 31, 1978
Atlanta Flames 6 Rangers 5 @ MSG (20–13–4)

The Blueshirts may have begun celebrating New Year's a little too early as they blew a three-goal lead in the third period and lost to the Atlanta Flames, 6–5, on New Year's Eve at Madison Square Garden.

The sellout crowd was enjoying an early party after Pat Hickey scored his 20th goal at the 34-second mark of the third period to give the Rangers a 5–2 lead. The diehards began a chant of "We want six," but it wasn't to be.

Atlanta scored three times in less than 10 minutes to tie the game, keyed by two goals from Eric Vail. The collapse was complete when Willi Plett scored with less than three minutes remaining in the game against Wayne Thomas, who had a rough third period, surrendering four goals on 11 shots.

Following two straight wins against Atlanta, the Rangers fell to 3–15–2 in their last 20 games against the Flames.

Eric Vail's two goals closed out 1978 on a bad note for the Blueshirts.
(Photo courtesy of Rdikeman at English Wikipedia [Public domain], via Wikimedia Commons)

CHAPTER 9
JANUARY: MURDER IN THE FIRST

The Rangers were under .500 (7–9) for the busy month of December. As the New Year arrived, the Blueshirts were tied (44 points) with the Philadelphia Flyers for second place in the Patrick Division. January began with a hot streak as the Rangers reeled off five straight wins.

Game 38, Wednesday, January 3, 1979
Rangers 6 Montreal Canadiens 2 @ MSG (21–13–4)

The Rangers had a good day, both on and off the ice.

Before the game, the National Hockey League reinstated suspended right wing Don Murdoch. The 22-year-old was serving a one-year suspension for being arrested on cocaine possession after his rookie season, but the Rangers submitted an application for reinstatement that was approved by the League.

Murdoch, who would officially become eligible to play after the Rangers' 40th game, was at Madison Square Garden for that night's game with the Montreal Canadiens who were riding a 15-game unbeaten (12 wins, three ties) streak, but the Rangers played their best game of the season in ending the Habs' run with a 6–2 victory.

Goals by Dave Maloney and Mike McEwen gave the

Rangers a 2–0 lead after one period. Guy Lafleur scored for Montreal to cut into the Rangers' lead but the Blueshirts blew the game wide open with goals by Nick Fotiu, Ron Duguay, and Ulf Nilsson to take a 5–1 lead into the second intermission.

Coach Fred Shero literally got into the action when a loose puck clipped him above his right eye. Shero's glasses broke and he was given several stitches.

For Shero's team, it was a much-needed solid performance to break them out of their recent malaise. "We have been playing well lately, except for third periods," Duguay said after the game. "We wanted to make sure that we didn't go into a shell and that we got out of our own end."

Game 39, Friday, January 5, 1979
Rangers 6 Vancouver Canucks 4 @MSG (22–13–4)

Ulf Nilsson scored his first NHL hat trick to power the Rangers past the Vancouver Canucks, 6–4, at Madison Square Garden.

Nilsson opened the scoring with his 15th goal of the season in the first period. With the score tied, 1–1, in the second period, Nilsson broke in alone on Canucks goaltender Dunc Wilson and scored his second goal of the game, short-handed, and the Rangers never looked back.

Walt Tkaczuk's 200th career goal gave the Rangers a 3–1 lead later in the period. Nilsson completed his hat trick midway through the third period.

Game 40, Tuesday, January 9, 1979
Rangers 5 @ St. Louis Blues 3 (23–13–4)

Three consecutive second-period goals by Anders Hedberg, Ron Duguay, and Ulf Nilsson led the Rangers to a 5–3 win over the Blues in St. Louis.

Despite outshooting the Blues, 18–4, the Blueshirts trailed, 2–1, after one period. Nilsson's fourth goal in the last two games was his 18th of the season. After the Blues cut the lead to 4–3 in the third, Duguay scored his second of the game and 13th of the season to put the game away for their third straight win.

Game 41, Wednesday, January 10, 1979
Rangers 5 @ Colorado Rockies 3 (24–13–4)

The Rangers fell behind early for the second straight game but rallied for a 5–3 win in Colorado to extend their winning streak to four.

This time the Rangers trailed 3–0 after one, but the red hot Ulf Nilsson began the comeback midway through the second period with his 19th goal. The Swedish center also extended his goal-scoring streak to four games.

Goals by Ron Duguay, Pierre Plante, and Anders Hedberg completed a second period where the Rangers took the lead with four unanswered goals.

In the third, Phil Esposito scored his 22nd goal to cap off an impressive come-from-behind win.

Don Murdoch played his first game since being reinstated from suspension. After the game he admitted there were some butterflies. "There was some nervousness there," he said.

Game 42, Sunday, January 14, 1979
Rangers 6 @ Atlanta Flames 4 (25–13–4)

In just his second game back from suspension, Don Murdoch scored a hat trick to lead the Rangers to their fifth straight victory as they scored a 6–4 win in Atlanta.

For the third straight game, the Rangers had to come from behind. Atlanta took a 3–0 lead after one and led 4–1 after two, but Murdoch scored his first goal of the season early in the third period to narrow the gap to 4–2.

Ulf Nilsson extended his goal-scoring streak to five straight games with his his 20th goal to make it a one-goal game. A little over eight minutes into the third period, Murdoch tied it up with his second goal. Less than five minutes later, the enigmatic winger completed his hat trick and give the Rangers a 5–4 lead.

Ron Duguay closed out the scoring with an empty-net goal to cap off a five-goal outburst in the final stanza. Murdoch also had an assist while Phil Esposito had a four-point night with a goal and three assists.

Getting a hat trick in his second game back off the suspension was just the elixir that Murdoch needed to get his season started. "I wanted to come back and prove that I can help this team," Murdoch said in a recent interview. "It [the hat trick] just gave me self-confidence for myself."

Game 43, Monday, January 15, 1979
Minnesota North Stars 8 Rangers 1 @ MSG (25–14–4)

For the second time this season, the Minnesota North Stars ended a lengthy Rangers win streak as they walloped them, 8–1, at Madison Square Garden. The loss snapped the Blueshirts' five-game win streak. The North Stars had earlier ended the Rangers' seven game win streak with a win at the Garden back on

November 8.

Minnesota's Tim Young joined the Islanders' Bryan Trottier (December 23) as the second opponent to have a five-goal game against the Rangers.

Don Murdoch, who made his home season debut, had some reservations about how he would be received by the hometown fans who were disappointed in him for the suspension. Rangers fans were well known for their passionate reverence for the team and as a group that wouldn't hesitate to let the players know how they felt about them. "You don't know if you're gonna step on the ice and you're gonna get booed or you're gonna step on the ice and they're gonna be behind ya," Murdoch said.

As it turned out, the fans were supportive as they gave him a nice ovation when he stepped on the Garden ice for the first time. "My stomach's turning, you know, and then to come out there and I got the warm reception, it just kind of made things easier," he said.

A warm reception at the Garden made things easier for Don Murdoch
(Photo courtesy of Joanna Ente)

Game 44, Wednesday January 17, 1979
Rangers 5 New York Islanders 3 @ MSG (26-14-4)

The Rangers scored five unanswered goals to beat the New York Islanders for the first time this season, 5-3, at Madison Square Garden.

After Mike Bossy gave the Islanders a 1–0 lead with his 37th goal just 1:09 into the game, Ron Greschner tied things up with a power play goal. In the second period, the Rangers scored three goals on ten shots to take a 4–1 lead after two. Ulf Nilsson scored his 21st goal to give the Rangers the lead, Ron Duguay scored his 16th, and Mike McEwen added his 12th with 15 seconds left in the period. Anders Hedberg added a third-period goal as the Rangers ended Islanders goaltender Chico Resch's 23-game unbeaten streak. Phil Esposito had two assists including the 800th of his career.

After the game, Islanders coach Al Arbour lamented his team's performance. "They outplayed us completely."

During the game, Pat Hickey garnered enough faith in his relationship with coach Fred Shero that he approached him about one of his pet peeves. Hickey told a story about how he was having a conversation about hockey with his father, who asked if he could find out "what Freddie is writing on that piece of paper" that he always carried around with him. Hickey said that he would find out.

"So, we're playing the Islanders, I'm having a good game, the team's playing well and I come off a shift and Freddie's pacing a little bit on the bench and then, I just leaned way back, took a big breath and yelled, 'Hey Fred, my dad wants to know what the hell are you writing down on that piece of paper,' and he says, 'Pat, that's just the way I mess everybody up. I don't write anything on it.' Just to keep everybody thinking.'"

Game 45, Saturday, January 20, 1979
@ St. Louis Blues 3 Rangers 2 (26–15–4)

Don Murdoch and Phil Esposito scored goals in a 3–2 loss in St. Louis. The Rangers outshot the Blues, 31–22, but couldn't get the tying goal past goaltender Ed Staniowski.

Game 46, Sunday, January 21, 1979
Rangers 5 Philadelphia Flyers 5 @ MSG (26–15–5)

Ulf Nilsson notched his second hat trick of the month, but the Rangers blew a 5–2 third period lead in a 5–5 tie with the Philadelphia Flyers at Madison Square Garden.

After Nilsson completed the hat trick with his 24th goal early in the third period, the Flyers scored the next three goals to tie the game. It was 5–4 when the Rangers went on a power play, but it was Philadephia that took advantage when Don Saleski scored a short-handed goal, his second of the game, to tie it up.

Game 47, Wednesday, January 24, 1979
@ Washington Capitals 5 Rangers 1 (26–16–5)

Ron Duguay's 17th goal was the Rangers' lone tally in a 5–1 loss to Washington at the Capital Centre that extended their winless streak to three games.

Game 48, Thursday January 25, 1979
Rangers 5 @ Buffalo Sabres 4 (27–16–5)

The Blueshirts scored a pair of third-period goals in a 21-second span to stun the Sabres in Buffalo, 5–4.

With the Rangers trailing, 4–3, entering the third, Ron Duguay set up Dave Maloney for the tying goal at 12:48, then Duguay's second goal of the game and 19th of the season gave the Rangers the lead for the first time.

John Davidson stopped 35 of 39 shots to pick up the win as the Rangers evened their record at 1–1 after two games of a six-game road trip.

Game 49, Saturday, January 27, 1979
Rangers 7 @ New York Islanders 2 (28–16–5)

Ulf Nilsson scored a goal and added four assists as the Rangers beat the New York Islanders, 7–2, at Nassau Coliseum. The win was made even sweeter as it ended the Islanders' streak of 28 consecutive regular season games at home without a loss, dating back to the previous season.

The Rangers took a 2–0 lead midway through the first period on goals by Mike McEwen and Nick Fotiu, who scored his third of the season.

Nilsson and Anders Hedberg, who scored the first of his two goals, gave the Rangers a 4–2 lead after two. In the third period, the Rangers scored three goals on 11 shots against goaltender Billy Smith, who was assessed three minor penalties during the game and gave up all seven goals on 33 shots.

Hedberg's second goal, his 21st, gave the Rangers a 5–2 lead. Ron Duguay scored his 20th and Pat Hickey added his 22nd to close out a very satisfying night for the Rangers. Dave Maloney said, "Let me say that, tonight at least, we were the better team."

The Rangers felt this was a statement game. Phil Esposito could sense that the team was starting to jell. "We're just this much short of being a great team," he said.

Game 50, Tuesday, January 30, 1979
Rangers 5 @ Vancouver Canucks 3 (29–16–5)

Ron Duguay extended his goal-scoring streak to four games and Phil Esposito scored two goals to lead the Rangers to a 5–3 victory over the Vancouver Canucks at Pacific Coliseum.

John Davidson made 44 saves, including 21 in a wild second period, as the Rangers made it three wins in four games during this six-game road trip.

Esposito's first goal of the game opened the scoring. Pat Hickey added his 22nd goal for a 2–0 lead after one.

Vancouver cut the lead in half in the second period but Anders Hedberg scored his 22nd to make it 3–1. In the third, Esposito scored his second goal of the game and 26th of the season while the red-hot Duguay netted his 21st for a 5–1 lead.

Game 51, Wednesday, January 31, 1979
@ Colorado Rockies 5 Rangers 4 (29–17–5)

A furious third-period comeback by the Rangers came up short in a 5–4 loss in Colorado that ended their three-game winning streak.

The Rockies led, 4–0, midway through the period before Anders Hedberg put the Rangers on the board with his 23rd goal of the season. Colorado upped the lead to 5–1 before the Rangers scored three goals in a 2:16 span to narrow the deficit to one.

Goals by Ron Duguay (who extended his goal-scoring streak to five games) Walt Tkaczuk, and Hedberg's second of the game with less than a minute left put the fans at McNichols Arena on edge, but the Rangers couldn't get the tying goal past Colorado goaltender Michel Plasse, who bested Wayne Thomas.

The Rangers outshot the Rockies, 42–22, including 16–7 in a wild third period, as they fell to 3–2 on their six-game road trip with one remaining.

Ron Duguay extended his goal-scoring streak to five games in a loss in Colorado
(Photo by Mark Rosenman)

CHAPTER 10
FEBRUARY: "POTVIN SUCKS"

The Rangers posted a 9–4–1 record in January and moved back into second place in the Patrick Division, 13 points behind the first place Islanders. The benchmark game of the regular season would take place in February and it spawned the famous "Potvin Sucks" chant that is still being heard 40 years later.

Game 52, Saturday, February 3, 1979
@ Los Angeles Kings 4 Rangers 2 (29–18–5)

Ron Duguay extended his streak of scoring a goal to six consecutive games but the Rangers dropped their second straight game to close out their six-game road trip with a 4–2 loss to the Kings.

Duguay's 23rd goal of the season gave the Rangers a 1–0 lead in the first period but the Kings scored a pair of third period goals to snap a 2–2 tie.

Game 53, Wednesday, February 14, 1979
Rangers 5 Boston Bruins 1 @ MSG (30–18–5)

Don Maloney made his NHL debut a successful one as he scored a goal and an added an assist to end the Bruins' nine-game winning streak at MSG as the Rangers walloped Boston, 5–1.

The 20-year-old Maloney was the Rangers' second-round pick (26th overall) in the 1978 NHL Amateur Draft. There was some doubt as to whether Dave Maloney's younger brother would be selected by the Rangers. When John Ferguson was general manager, he made it clear that he wanted him, but Fred Shero was now calling the shots and the Rangers had already dealt away their first-rounder (#7 overall) to Philadelphia as compensation for hiring their new coach and GM, and the Flyers chose Ken Linseman with the pick.

Maloney said brother Dave made a call in his behalf. "He made a call or two to whomever and he said the Rangers still had some interest in me. I certainly didn't expect to be a first-round pick, so my one hope is that I go to the Rangers after. The draft was in Montreal and at that time, Alan Eagleson was my agent. I remember when they signed Fred Shero, the Rangers lost the first-round pick and so the Rangers weren't picking again until the middle of the second round and I think was 26th. Mike Penny, who was a longtime hockey exec, was the GM of the Kitchener team I was playing on told me he thought I'd go in the middle of the second round or early third. I remember the conversation with him and I said so the Rangers just happened to pick right in that range, and sure enough, the Rangers drafted me, which was such a real big thrill for me."

The young left wing didn't waste time in endearing himself to Rangers fans as he scored his first NHL goal on his first shot to open the scoring a little over five minutes into the first period. "I was lucky enough to score on that first shot, you know, anytime you're a young player, you score, you know, that's to be a shot of confidence and energy," he said recently. Phil Esposito scored his 27th goal of the season and Ulf Nilsson added his 26th to give the Rangers a 3–0 lead after a first period in which the home team held the Bruins without a shot on goal.

Carol Vadnais and Pat Hickey extended the lead to 5–0 before John Davidson saw his shutout bid spoiled with just over five minutes remaining in the game.

The younger Maloney played left wing on a line with Esposito and Don Murdoch. "There just seemed to be instant chemistry between the three of us at the time was we all contributed," Maloney said. "Obviously, Phil was a star and a score and I knew if I could get him the puck anywhere around the net, that there is a pretty good chance he's going to put it in and Donnie Murdoch had that combination that he could score but could also make plays and, you know, he was coming off the suspension and the line just sort of clicked instantly."

It was a big night for the Maloney family, many of whom were on hand to watch Don and Dave play. "My mom and dad came down for it and my uncle and aunt, it was a blur thinking about it," Don Maloney said. "It was MSG, obviously, Dave was, as captain, and just the whole aura of being at the Garden on the ice against the Bruins, it was amazing, and somehow everything just started to click."

Game 54, Thursday, February 15, 1979
@ Buffalo Sabres 4 Rangers 3 (30–19–5)

In what may have been their most frustrating loss of the season, the Rangers dropped a 4–3 decision to the Sabres in Buffalo.

The Blueshirts not only lost the game, they lost defenseman Ron Greschner to a sprained shoulder when he collided with former Flyers tough guy Dave Schultz. Coach Fred Shero had only dressed five defensemen for the game so when the collision occurred early in the first period, the Rangers were down to four for the remainder of the contest.

Greschner was carried off the ice on a stretcher and was taken to Buffalo General Hospital after what he called "the hardest I've ever been hit playing hockey."

Don Murdoch scored two goals in the second period to give the Rangers a 3–2 lead after two periods but the Sabres scored a pair of third-period goals to take a one-goal lead. Buffalo goaltender Don Edwards stood tall in the final five minutes as the Rangers stormed the net but failed to get the tying goal.

John Davidson, who made 26 saves, said the Rangers' third consecutive road loss was hard to fathom. "Everybody worked hard on both teams, they just got one more. It happens," he said.

Game 55, Saturday, February 17, 1979
Rangers 4 @ Philadelphia Flyers 2 (31–19–5)

The Rangers' three-game road losing streak came to an end as they got past the Flyers, 4–2, at the Spectrum in Philadelphia.

Eddie Johnstone, Ulf Nilsson, and Ron Duguay scored third-period goals to power the Rangers in a game that saw Flyers goaltender Bernie Parent suffer a career-ending eye injury in the first period. Flyers defenseman Jimmy Watson's stick caught Parent in the eye during a Rangers scoring chance.

The stick went through the eyehole of the future Hall of Famer's mask. Parent ripped the mask off and headed to the locker room.

Wayne Stephenson replaced Parent in goal and took a 1–0

lead into the third period, but the Rangers scored four times to earn the win with Pat Hickey's empty-net goal capping off the scoring.

Wayne Thomas made 30 saves for the win. The 31-year-old veteran netminder was part of a three-goalie rotation (along with John Davidson and Doug Soetaert) that Shero used during the regular season. "I was part of a three-goalie system in Montreal. It wasn't that uncommon actually in the '70s," according to Thomas. "The biggest, toughest part of the three-goalie system is if you're decent people, sharing the net and, you know, and wanting to share the net. I mean we got along really well with the others, still great friends, but the practices is the toughest time."

Thomas said the arrangement made it tough to stay sharp. "If you had to wait your turn, three guys and you want the team to win, I mean you can be two to three weeks or a month before you get back in there, before somebody else screwed up your turn [came up] again, and that's not what you want, you know, it's hard enough with two, we got three."

Johnstone, who tied the game with his fourth goal of the season, said it was a tough season for him personally because he wasn't in the lineup every night. "That season I dressed for only 30 games and I was never hurt, so it was a very, very hard year. I can't tell you how many times I dressed for warm-ups and then got the hook but that was just the way it was."

This game was in Philadelphia, so Johnstone knew he would play. "I always played in Philly and Boston, the tougher teams. I always seemed to play against them.

Even with the inconsistent ice time, Johnstone respected Shero. "Freddie never made me feel like I was a 'black ace' (nickname for a spare player who was a healthy scratch). I participated in every practice and I did the same stuff as everybody else. At the end of the practice, if I didn't want to stay on the ice, I wasn't forced to stay. He treated me really good and I think he respected me because of the way I worked. I know I gave it all I had every shift, so I think he respected that."

Game 56, Sunday, February 18, 1979
Rangers 6 Washington Capitals 6 @ MSG (31–19–6)

In a seesaw game that saw Phil Esposito net a record–setting 30th career hat trick, the Rangers played to a 6–6 tie with the Washington Capitals at the Garden.

Esposito's first goal of the game in the first period tied the game, 1–1. The Blueshirts trailed, 5–4, after a wild second period that saw a total of seven goals scored. Don Murdoch, Ron Duguay, and Steve Vickers all scored but the Rangers still trailed by a goal.

Esposito's 30th goal of the season in the third period, his third of the night, gave the Rangers a 6–5 lead but Washington's Rolf Edberg scored with less than six minutes left to tie the game.

Game 57, Wednesday, February 21, 1979
Rangers 7 St. Louis Blues 3 @ MSG (32–19–6)

The Rangers scored five goals in the third period as they topped the St. Louis Blues in a wild 7–3 win at Madison Square Garden. The game featured a brawl in the third period when both benches emptied in what became a 10-minute melee.

The game was tied early in the third period before goals by Dave Maloney, Carol Vadnais, and Phil Esposito in a 1:35 span gave the Rangers a 6–3 lead. Mike McEwen, Don Maloney, Mario Marois, and Dean Talafous scored the other Ranger goals.

The Blueshirts outshot the Blues, 50–19, including a 22–4

advantage in the final stanza.

The brawl began after Blues left wing Brian Sutter scored his third goal of the game to make it 3–3. Nick Fotiu used the traditional method of challenging Blues enforcer Steve Durbano to a fight when he dropped his stick. Durbano did not drop his stick and swung it at Fotiu, who was enraged even more as he tried to get away from linesman John D'Amico, who was holding him back.

Both teams were milling around on the ice when Durbano suddenly skated across the ice to get at Fotiu who was standing by the Rangers bench. As the two came to blows, other players followed and got into a number of scrums.

When things finally settled down, Durbano skated off to the dressing room, but not before he mooned the Garden crowd. Fotiu also left the ice, as the crowd chanted, "We want Nick," but he reportedly went towards Durbano under the stands. A few Rangers, including Phil Esposito and Dave Maloney, followed their teammate while some Blues players also tried to get in the entrance where the home team came on the ice.

Durbano, who was assessed a near-record 45 minutes of penalty time, including 35 in the third period, was handed a five-game suspension by the NHL two days later. Fotiu, who received a ten-minute penalty as well as a game misconduct, was fined $300 by the league.

Game 58, Saturday, February 24, 1979
Rangers 4 @ Toronto Maple Leafs 2 (33–19–6)

Don Murdoch scored twice including the tiebreaking goal in the third period to lead the Rangers to a 4–2 win over the Toronto Maple Leafs at Maple Leaf Gardens.

For the second straight game the Rangers poured it on the opposition's net as they fired 49 shots at Mike Palmateer.

Murdoch's second goal of the game, and ninth of the season, gave the Rangers a 3–2 lead with less than six minutes remaining. Phil Esposito added his 32nd for insurance.

Don Maloney had three assists but a mistake that he made early in the game led to a demonstration of how Fred Shero quietly instilled confidence in his players. "I remember in my sixth game in Toronto, turning the puck over and not clearing the puck and leading to a scoring chance or I took a bad penalty. I remember coming back to the bench and then, at that time you're just trying to survive, let alone do something positive. What I do remember was Fred coming down the bench. He'd come down just to pat me on the back and said, 'Keep working, just keep working, we believe in you,' that kind of thing. It was all very subtle, very quiet. It wasn't a big speech, it was just a soft word. There was never ever any yelling and screaming and threatening, which could happen back in that era. So he had a very subtle way of getting the message across and obviously, we had a very strong team and he was the right coach at the right time."

This game marked the only one that defenseman Dean Turner played that season. Turner had been playing with the New Haven Nighthawks of the AHL when he was called up to make his NHL debut.

"We came in on a plane and we were getting bounced all over the place," Turner recalled. "I'll never forget, I was sitting kind of "kitty corner" to Espo and Phil's looking around like 'Man, this is bullshit.' It was so bad that we had to like come in a couple of times and then take off again, come in and take off."

Game 59, Sunday, February 25, 1979
Rangers 3 New York Islanders 2 @ MSG (34–19–6)

February 25, 1979 was a seminal date in Rangers history as it marked the birth of the infamous "Potvin Sucks" chant that would be heard at Madison Square Garden for years to come.

The Rangers beat the Islanders, 3–2, but lost center Ulf Nilsson in the process when he suffered a broken ankle as a result of a check by future Hall of Fame defenseman Denis Potvin. The incident took place late in the first period when Nilsson went to play the puck in the corner. As the Swedish center pivoted around, Potvin checked him hard into the boards. Nilsson stayed down on the ice with a fractured ankle and was never the same player when he did return.

Nilsson recently said he did not realize the severity of the injury at the time. "Yeah, I didn't know how bad it was, but yeah, I probably tore a lot of the ligaments," he said. It was a huge loss for the Rangers because he was having a terrific season, averaging a point per game before he got hurt. "Up until that point, I probably had one of my best seasons as a professional hockey player," said Nilsson.

No penalty was called, and Potvin thought the hit was clean. "Definitely, I hit him clean. I got him with my shoulder and I got him high," he said after the game.

Potvin would forever draw the wrath of the Ranger fans whenever he played at the Garden. Even after he retired and was long gone from the NHL, the chant is still heard to this very day. "Potvin Sucks" was a parody of a rallying cry entitled, "Let's Go Band." The short, catchy tune would begin with an instrumental beat and conclude with the three words, "Let's go band."

Later in the game, the Garden organist played the instrumental part of "Let's Go Band" and Rangers fans ended it in unison with "Potvin Sucks." Garden officials did not want to encourage the fans to recite the chant so they stopped playing it, but some fans took it upon themselves to use a high pitch whistle for the instrumental part to lead into the "Potvin Sucks" chant.

"I always thought that Ranger fans were yelling "Potvin's cups" and holding up four fingers," Potvin said during a recent radio interview.

Potvin said he felt the wrath of the Ranger fans for a very long time after that. "It wasn't easy in the beginning," Potvin said. "Believe me, when I'm standing on the blue line for the National Anthem and when I feel this nine-volt battery go by my ear, you realize there was hatred at the time. The last few years, when I was broadcasting for that team in the south, [Florida Panthers] coming into Madison Square Garden, people would yell 'Potvin sucks' with a big smile on their face. It's become a chant that everybody sings along. I'm not so sure everybody knows what it really means or why or how it started, so, I just wish I could get paid for it."

Potvin's cups or Potvin sucks?
(Photo courtesy Charny[CC BY-SA 3.0, from Wikimedia Commons)

Dean Talafous's second-period goal proved to be the game-winner. The Rangers held the Islanders without a shot in the second period and ended Mike Bossy's NHL-record 10-game goalscoring streak as they beat their hated rivals.

The score was not indicative of how much the Rangers dominated the contest. After the game, losing goaltender Chico Resch said, "They deserved to win by a much bigger score than 3–2." The victory gave the Rangers 74 points, one more than they had accumulated the entire previous season.

Doug Soetaert, who started in net in place of John Davidson, who injured his shoulder in the previous game against the St.Louis

Blues, made 14 saves to earn the win. As far as being the goaltender who stopped Bossy's streak, Soetaert said, "If Bossy had scored and we won, I wouldn't care."

Game 60, Tuesday, February 27, 1979
@ St. Louis Blues 4 Rangers 1 (34–20–6)

The Blues jumped to a 3–0 lead after one period and never looked back as they downed the Rangers, 4–2, in St. Louis.

Don Murdoch broke up Ed Staniowski's shutout bid with a goal late in the second period. Murdoch's older brother Bob scored the fourth goal for St. Louis. There was no retaliation for the bench-clearing brawl that occurred between the teams six days earlier in New York.

After 60 games, the Rangers sat in second place in the Patrick Division with 74 points, 14 points behind the first-place Islanders.

Game 61, Wednesday, February 28, 1979
Rangers 4 @ Minnesota North Stars 4 (34–20–7)

Playing their second game in as many nights, the Rangers appeared to be fatigued as they let a two-goal lead slip away and had to settle for a 4–4 tie with the Minnesota North Stars at Metropolitan Sports Center.

Goals by Eddie Johnstone, Phil Esposito (his 33rd), and Pat Hickey had given the Rangers a 3–1 lead after one period but the Blues tied the game with a pair of goals in the second period.

The Rangers regained the lead as Don Murdoch scored early in the third period but Minnesota tied the game once again as the Rangers settled for a point.

Before 94: The Story of the 1978-79 New York Rangers

CHAPTER 11
MARCH/APRIL: HEADIN' TOWARDS THE PLAYOFFS

The Rangers headed into the final portion of the regular season in third place in the Patrick Division, one point behind the second-place Atlanta Flames, but with two games in hand. The top six teams in the Clarence Campbell Conference would qualify for the playoffs.

Game 62, Saturday, March 3, 1979
Rangers 2 Buffalo Sabres 2 @ MSG (34-20-8)

Dean Talafous scored midway through the third period as the Rangers salvaged a 2-2 tie with the Buffalo Sabres at Madison Square Garden, extending their winless streak to four games.

Game 63, Sunday, March 4, 1979
Toronto Maple Leafs 4 Rangers 2 @ MSG (34-21-8)

It was the Rangers' fate to run into an emotional Toronto Maple Leafs team as they dropped a 4-2 decision to them at Madison Square Garden.

Leafs coach Roger Neilson returned one day after he was fired by team owner Harold Ballard. The players rallied together and demanded that Neilson to be reinstated, so he was back behind the bench against a team that he would eventually coach more than a decade later.

Two Toronto goals less than a minute apart in the second period gave the Leafs a 3–0 lead. Goals by Don Murdoch and Steve Vickers drew the home team close in the third period, but they were now winless in their last five games.

Game 64, Wednesday, March 7, 1979
Rangers 5 Colorado Rockies 3 @ MSG (35–21–8)

The Rangers snapped their five-game winless skid with a 5–3 victory over the Colorado Rockies at Madison Square Garden.

Pat Hickey and Walt Tkaczuk keyed a four-goal first period by scoring within a 14-second span. Pierre Plante and Dean Talafous rounded out the first-period outburst. Phil Esposito's 34th goal closed out the scoring in the third period.

Mike McEwen added two assists as the Rangers moved past the Atlanta Flames for second place in the Patrick Division.

Due to a number of injuries to their defensemen, the Rangers called up Andre Dore from New Haven to make his NHL debut. Dore, who grew up in Montreal and was a fourth-round selection (60th overall) in the 1978 NHL Amateur Draft, skated with a kiddie corps of defensemen that included 22-year-olds Dave Maloney, Dave Farrish, and Mike McEwen and fellow 21-year-old Mario Marois.

Looking back, Dore said he was not in awe of Madison Square Garden as he would've been had he been American born. "I just told myself I'm going to get out there and I'm just going to skate, skate, skate and I'm just gonna act like I belong," he said.

He didn't want to let this opportunity slip by, even at the risk of being hurt. "I took a shot on the foot in the very first period and I was afraid of taking my skate off because I didn't know if my foot was broken," Dore said. "I didn't think so but I said if I take my skate off, I'll never be able to put it back on. I remembered the trainer wanted me to open my skate and I said, 'No I can't' and I told him why. So he slapped a bag of ice on the outside of my skate. That's the only time I've ever seen that. We go on to win the game and then they tell me I'm going to Montreal. So I'm excited as hell and I'm scared as hell too because my foot has blown up and I can't tell anyone you know. I'm limping badly but there's no way I'm going to say anything to anybody. I'm going to play that next game. I'm going to find a way to play that game in Montreal."

Game 65, Saturday, March 10, 1979
Rangers 6 @ Montreal Canadiens 3 (36–21–8)

The Blueshirts made it three-for-three against Montreal this season as they scored a 6–3 win, their second in Montreal. They won their second in a row overall and fourth straight versus the Canadiens dating back to last season. "Maybe we should play them more often," Fred Shero joked after the game.

The Rangers led, 2–1, after one period on goals by Walt Tkaczuk and Pat Hickey. Ron Duguay's 26th goal snapped a 2–2 tie in the second period. "I think we're psyched a little more playing against them," Duguay said afterwards.

Anders Hedberg scored a power play goal to give the Rangers a 4–2 lead and Lucien DeBlois scored twice, including the final goal against goalie Michel "Bunny" Larocque. Montreal's starting goaltender, Ken Dryden, gave up the first five Ranger goals before he pulled a leg muscle and left the game in the third period.

Dore had the thrill of a lifetime by playing the second of the two games that he would play that season in his hometown. "You can go to the Forum a thousand times and think you know exactly what the rink looks like and feels like and smells like," Dore said, "and when you're actually dressed to play there, nothing is the way you think it is."

During the warmups, Dore recognized many familiar faces in the stands. "I see all these people looking at me and I'm not processing it but they're all people I've grown up with."

When the game was over, so was Dore's short tenure with the NHL club that season. "Somebody from the Rangers comes up and gives me an airplane ticket and says, 'Thank you, New Haven's playing in Halifax tomorrow, so they expect you at the game.' I mean it was like *Holy shit*, you know, like you don't know that's coming at all, and right there, in that second, you go from the highest high of playing the game in the Forum to the low of getting your plane ticket, knowing you're not getting on the airplane back to New York, but, instead you're getting on an airplane to Halifax."

Game 66, Sunday, March 11, 1979
Rangers 5 Chicago Black Hawks 2 @ MSG (37–21–8)

The Maloney brothers each scored a goal and an assist to lead the Rangers to a 5–2 win over the Chicago Black Hawks at Madison Square Garden for their third consecutive win.

Goals by Walt Tkaczuk and Ron Duguay gave the Rangers a 2–1 lead after two periods. In the third, Don Maloney set up Phil Esposito's 35th goal, a power play tally, for a 3–1 lead. After Chicago cut the deficit to 3–2, Don Maloney scored to make it 4–2. Brother Dave scored with less than a minute left to close out the scoring.

Don and brother Dave Maloney each had a goal and an assist in the Rangers' 4–2 win over the Chicago Black Hawks
(Photo by Mark Rosenman)

Game 67, Wednesday, March 14, 1979
Atlanta Flames 6 Rangers 4 @ MSG (37–22–8)

Atlanta beat the Rangers, 6–4, for their sixth straight win at Madison Square Garden. The win moved the Flames one point behind the second–place Rangers in the Patrick Division.

The Rangers let two leads get away. Goals by Don Murdoch in the first period and Mario Marois in the second gave the Rangers a 2–0 lead after two but the Flames scored three unanswered goals to grab a 3–2 lead. Bob Murdoch, Don's brother, got Atlanta's first goal of the game.

Don Maloney tied the game late in the second period and the

Rangers took a 4–3 lead early in the third on a goal by Walt Tkaczuk, who scored for a fourth consecutive game. Atlanta came back to tie it on a goal by Bill Clement. Bob Murdoch's second assist of the game set up Jean Pronovost's game-winning goal. Pronovost added an insurance goal with 33 seconds remaining.

Game 68, Thursday, March 15, 1979
Rangers 7 @ Boston Bruins 4 (38–22–8)

Phil Esposito scored four goals for the fifth time in his illustrious career as the Rangers beat his old team, the Boston Bruins, 7-4, at Boston Garden.

Espo scored twice, including a power play goal to open the scoring, as the Rangers took a 2–0 lead and never looked back. Former Ranger Rick Middleton put Boston on the board, but the Rangers led, 2–1, after one period.

Goals by Walt Tkaczuk, who extended his goalscoring streak to five games, and Mike McEwen, his 16th of the season, gave the Rangers a 4–1 lead after two.

In the third period, Wayne Cashman scored for the Bruins to cut the deficit to two goals, but Esposito's third goal of the game gave him his 31st career hat trick and the Rangers a 5–2 lead. Esposito was actually trying to pass the puck, but it hit the skates of Bruins defenseman Dick Redmond and went into the net past Boston goaltender Jim Pettie.

Anders Hedberg set up Don Murdoch's goal with his third assist of the game and Esposito completed the Ranger scoring with his fourth goal of the night and 39th of the season.

Game 69, Saturday, March 17, 1979
@ New York Islanders 5 Rangers 2 (38–23–8)

Mike Bossy scored his 58th goal as the New York Islanders opened a 16-point lead in the Patrick Division after they beat the Rangers, 5–2, at Nassau Coliseum on St. Patrick's Day.

The Islanders scored just 15 seconds into the game and never looked back. Walt Tkaczuk scored a goal for a sixth consecutive game while Mike McEwen had the other Ranger goal

Mike Bossy's 58th spoiled the Rangers St. Patrick's Day
Photo Courtesy of New York Islanders/NHL
[Public domain], via Wikimedia Commons

Game 70, Sunday, March 18, 1979
@ Pittsburgh Penguins 5 Rangers 1 (38–24–8)

Pittsburgh Penguins defenseman Ron Stackhouse scored a hat trick to hand the Rangers a 5–1 loss at Civic Arena. It was the Rangers' second straight loss and their third in the last four games.

It was the first (and would be the only) career hat trick for

the nine-year veteran who scored all three of his goals on the power play.

Don Maloney's sixth goal of the season tied the game, 1–1, late in the first period, but Pittsburgh scored four unanswered goals, three by Stackhouse, to secure two points.

Game 71, Tuesday, March 20, 1979
Rangers 2 @ Washington Capitals 2 (38–24–9)

Phil Esposito's 40th goal of the season couldn't have come at a better time as he scored with five seconds left in the game to give the Rangers a 2–2 tie with the Washington Capitals at Capital Centre.

With goaltender Doug Soetaert on the bench for an extra attacker, Esposito put the puck past Jim Bedard as the clock wound down. The point gave the Rangers a three-point lead over the Philadelphia Flyers for second place in the Patrick Division.

Game 72, Wednesday, March 21, 1979
Rangers 7 @ Chicago Black Hawks 6 (39–24–9)

Anders Hedberg scored twice, including his 30th goal, the Maloney brothers both scored in the same game, and Phil Esposito added his 41st goal to lead the Rangers to a wild 7–6 win at Chicago Stadium.

The game was tied, 1–1, after one period but the Rangers exploded for 16 shots and three goals from Dave Maloney, Phil Esposito, and Lucien DeBlois to open a 4–1 lead after two.

A total of eight goals were scored in a crazy third period. Hedberg's first of the game gave the Rangers a 5–1 lead but Chicago narrowed the gap to 5–3. Hedberg's second of the game and 30th of the season restored a three–goal lead before the Black Hawks scored again as they tried to rally.

Pat Hickey's 29th gave the Rangers a 7–4 lead and Chicago scored twice in the final three minutes to cement the final score. Chicago fired 45 shots at Wayne Thomas, including 22 in the third period.

Game 73, Sunday, March 25, 1979
Montreal Canadiens 1 Rangers 0 @ MSG (39–25–9)

Yvon Lambert's second period goal was the only score of the game, as the Canadiens beat the Rangers for the first time this season. Montreal goaltender Michel Larocque made 25 saves while Doug Soetaert stopped 29 of 30 shots.

Game 74, Tuesday, March 27,1979
Rangers 4 Philadelphia Flyers 4 @ MSG (39-25-10)

The Rangers blew a 4–0 second period lead and had to settle for a disappointing 4–4 tie with the Philadelphia Flyers at Madison Square Garden.

Goals from Mike McEwen, Don Murdoch, Lucien DeBlois, and Anders Hedberg had given the Rangers a 4–0 lead midway through the second period. Future Hall of Famer Bill Barber's goal late in the second period seemed to get the Flyers going and they carried that momentum into the third period when they scored three times to tie it up.

Rangers leading scorer Phil Esposito took a shot off of his foot in the third period and left the game.

Game 75, Wednesday, March 28, 1979
@ Pittsburgh 7 Rangers 1 (39–26–10)

The Blueshirts ran into a red-hot Pittsburgh Penguins team and could not slow them down as they were walloped, 7–1, in Pittsburgh.

Center Greg Malone scored a hat trick as the Penguins clinched a playoff berth and ran their unbeaten streak to ten games. Anders Hedberg scored the lone goal for the Rangers, who were thoroughly outplayed and outshot, 42–29.

Game 76, Sunday, April 1, 1979
@ Philadelphia Flyers 7 Rangers 3 (39–27–10)

The Rangers continued their poor play of late and were blown out for a second straight game as they dropped a 7–3 decision to the Flyers in Philadelphia despite two goals by Pat Hickey.

The Blueshirts, 1–5–2 in their last eight games, fell five points behind Philadelphia for second place in the Patrick Division but remained one point ahead of fourth-place Atlanta with four to play.

Goaltender John Davidson returned to the ice after missing the entire month of March with a shoulder injury but did not finish the game and was replaced by Wayne Thomas.

Game 77, Monday, April 2, 1979
Rangers 5 Los Angeles Kings 4 @ MSG (40–27–10)

Pat Hickey scored twice for the second straight game, Phil Esposito added his 42nd of the season, and the Rangers picked up a huge 5–4 victory over the Los Angeles Kings at Madison Square Garden.

The game didn't start on a good note for the Rangers as they surrendered a goal while skating with a 5-on-3 advantage. Center Butch Goring scored the short-handed goal on a breakaway to give Los Angeles a 1–0 lead in the first period.

Walt Tkaczuk scored his 15th goal of the season to tie the game and Hickey's first of the game and 32nd of the season gave the Rangers a 2–1 lead after one period.

Hickey's second goal of the game to snapped a 2–2 tie in the second period and Ron Greschner scored his 17th for a 4–2 lead. Kings center Marcel Dionne's 57th cut the lead to 4–3 after two periods.

Phil Esposito's 42nd upped the lead to 5-3 in the third period before the Kings closed the scoring as Goring scored his second of the game.

With three games to play, and a home-and-home series up next against the Flames, the Rangers led Atlanta by three points for third place in the Patrick Division.

Game 78, Wednesday, April 4, 1979
Rangers 3 Atlanta Flames 3 @ MSG (40–27–11)

In the first game of a crucial home-and-home series, the Rangers played to a 3–3 tie with the Atlanta Flames at Madison Square Garden. The Blueshirts maintained their three-point lead over Atlanta for second place in the Patrick Division with two games remaining in the regular season.

Pat Hickey's 34th goal gave the Rangers a 3–2 lead in the third period, but Atlanta tied the game on a power play goal by Ken Houston that allowed the Flames to extend their unbeaten streak at the Garden to seven games.

Mike McEwen became the third defenseman (Brad Park and Ron Greschner were the other two) in Ranger history to score 20 goals in a season when he tipped in a shot from Mario Marois in the second period.

Game 79, Friday, April 6, 1979
@ Atlanta Flames 9 Rangers 2 (40–28–11)

Don Maloney scored the only two Ranger goals as they were trounced in Atlanta, 9–2. The Flames moved to within one point of the third-place Rangers in the Patrick Division.

John Davidson continued to struggle after returning from injury and was replaced by Doug Soetaert after allowing seven goals.

Game 80, Sunday, April 8, 1979
New York Islanders 5 Rangers 2 @ MSG (40–29–11)

The Rangers finished the regular season with a disappointing 5–2 loss to the New York Islanders at Madison Square Garden.

Despite the defeat, the Rangers clinched third place in the Patrick Division with 91 points as Atlanta lost at Philadelphia, 4–2. The Flyers ended up four points ahead of the Rangers for second place. Mike Bossy scored his 68th and 69th goals of the season as the Rangers closed out the regular season with just two wins in their last 12 games.

The victory gave the Islanders the distinction of having the league's best record with 116 points and a bye in the preliminary round. It was the final regular season meeting between the rivals and the end of the opening act for what would be one of the biggest upsets in Stanley Cup playoff history.

Phil Esposito and Anders Hedberg led the team in scoring with 78 points. Esposito led the way with 42 goals while Hedberg had a team-high 45 assists. John Davidson led the goaltenders with 20 wins and a 3.53 goal-against average.

CHAPTER 12
"PRELIMINARY ROUND: STEP ONE"

The Rangers were hoping the third time in the best-of-three preliminary round would be a charm. The previous two times, the Rangers suffered the infamous crushing defeat in sudden-death overtime of the third and deciding game against the Islanders in 1975 while also losing a three-game series the previous season to the Buffalo Sabres.

According to the way the playoffs were structured, the Rangers would play a best-of-three preliminary round against the Los Angeles Kings. The four first-place teams (New York Islanders, Montreal Canadiens, Boston Bruins, and Chicago Black Hawks) received byes and the remaining eight qualifiers were seeded according to points. The Rangers were seeded second and were matched with seventh-seed LA, who had finished third in the Norris Division with a 34–34–12 record (80 points).

Late in the season, Dean Talafous suffered a neck injury that would keep him out of the playoffs. Talafous wanted to play so badly that he got up out of a hospital bed and went to Garden to dress for the final game of the regular season.

"So literally Anders Hedberg had to drive me down in my van, because I couldn't even sit up I was in so much pain," Talafous said. "I laid down in the back of the van, drove down, got dressed, went out, tried to hit everything that moved, made it through to like the second period and was right back in the hospital."

John Davidson's shoulder injury was a concern going into the playoffs. "I had fallen down with my arm extended and that was just it, I don't know, it just sort of pulled it back and that was pretty sore but it wasn't a separation or dislocation," Davidson said. "It was a seven-to-ten-day job and I hadn't played the entire month of March and I played in four games before the playoffs."

Game 1, Tuesday, April 10, 1979
Rangers 7 Los Angeles Kings 1 @ MSG
Rangers lead series, 1–0

During the regular season, the Rangers won three of four meetings against the Los Angeles Kings, scoring 20 goals in those three victories. The pattern continued in the opener of the preliminary round. Mike McEwen's power play goal snapped a 1–1 tie in the first period and the Rangers never looked back as they walloped LA, 7–1, at the Garden to grab Game 1.

Despite the lopsided score, John Davidson was a big reason why the Blueshirts led the series one game to none.

Davidson, who made 31 saves, had not played much down the stretch of the regular season because of a shoulder injury but he was stout in the first postseason game. "They had as many good chances as we did," said Walt Tkaczuk. "Ours went in and theirs didn't because J.D. stopped them." Even the opposition had to tip their cap to him. "Sometimes a hot goaltender turns things around and that's what Davidson did tonight," said Kings center, future Ranger and Hall of Famer Marcel Dionne.

During a recent interview, Davidson admitted to having butterflies at the start. "I'm frankly pretty nervous because I don't know where my game is after not playing for two weeks hardly."

The Rangers goaltender got a huge break early in a scoreless game after Kings left wing Charlie Simmer broke in all alone. Simmer made a move that faked Davidson out of his skates and left the net empty, but his shot hit the outside of the post to keep the game scoreless. "He comes down the wall to my right," Davidson said. "I move out at him, he goes around me, empty net and he hits the goal post."

That was a huge play and a turning point for Davidson who was concerned how his shoulder would react to game conditions and he got tested right away. "They hit the post and then I really felt that the luck was there and from that point on in the game, I played well, our team played great," Davidson said. "We scored seven and then we went into Los Angeles and won there."

A little over two minutes later, Lucien DeBlois brought the excited Garden crowd to its feet as he scored on the power play for a 1–0 lead. After Simmer tied the game with a power play goal of his own, McEwen scored yet another power play goal, off a faceoff win, for a lead that the Rangers never relinquished. Tkaczuk beat Dionne on the draw and got the puck back to the Ranger defenseman, who was not looking to shoot. "Somebody came out at me and I was going to pass, but he turned away, so I walked in for the shot," McEwen said after the game.

Steve Vickers completed a two-on-one rush by tipping in a shot from Tkaczuk that gave the Rangers a 3–1 lead and began a four-goal outburst in the second period. Dave Maloney scored his first of two, Ron Greschner, and Tkaczuk also scored their first goals of the postseason and the Rangers had a 6–1 lead after two periods of play. Maloney's second of the game rounded out the scoring in the third period.

The Maloney brothers tallied three points in Game 1 against the LA Kings. (Photo courtesy of New York Rangers)

Kings rookie goaltender Mario Lessard allowed seven goals on 30 shots. The Rangers were three-for-three on the power play and killed off five of six Los Angeles power play opportunities. "You have to give our power play and penalty killing units a lot of credit tonight," Davidson said.

Game 2, Thursday, April 12, 1979
Rangers 2 @ Los Angeles Kings 1 (OT)
Rangers win series, 2–0

Phil Esposito lived by the credo, "If at first you don't succeed, try, try again."

Esposito missed wide on a breakaway in overtime that would've won the game but he didn't miss on his second try. "I don't think I can count one hand when I've missed those kind of shots," Esposito said after it was over. A little more than three minutes later, Espo scored the game-winner, his second goal of the night, as the Rangers beat the Kings, 2–1, to win the preliminary round series, two games to none.

John Davidson was superb for a second consecutive game with 35 saves, including three in overtime. The Kings scored a power play goal in the first period and held the lead until Esposito's first goal at 1:11 of the third period tied the game.

Going into overtime, the Rangers had a chance to advance or they could allow the Kings back into the series and have it come down to a one-game showdown. Mario Marois said the room was quiet while awaiting the start of overtime. "Nobody wants to give the other team a chance to come back."

Don Maloney never had a doubt that the Rangers would win. "I didn't think at any time that we were going to lose that series, myself," he said. "We were a good team on a roll."

Esposito scored the winning goal off a perfect feed from Don Maloney as he was able to poke the puck past Mario Lessard despite being checked by defenseman Darryl Edestrand. "I had my stick loose on the ice," Esposito said, "even if I had someone wrapped around me, Maloney made a perfect pass."

Phil Esposito scored the overtime winner to close out the Kings.
(Photo courtesy of New York Rangers)

Next up, the Rangers would meet the Philadelphia Flyers in the quarterfinals.

CHAPTER 13
QUARTERFINALS: FREDDIE'S REVENGE

The last time the Rangers met the Flyers in the playoffs was in the 1974 semifinals. Fred Shero was behind the opposite bench then as the Rangers lost a heartbreaking and punishing seven-game series.

Philadelphia went on to win their first Stanley Cup, but for the Rangers, the series will always be remembered for the beating that defenseman Dale Rolfe took from Flyers tough guy Dave Schultz in the first period of the seventh game. The Rangers were severely criticized for their lack of a response and now they had a chance to gain a measure of revenge.

A nasty preseason incident became a reference point, even though two of the participants, Flyers rookie left wing Jim Cunningham and Rangers left wing Frank Beaton, were not even with their respective teams for the quarterfinal series.

That melee began when Rangers' left wing Nick Fotiu fought Cunningham. Recalling the fight, Beaton said Fotiu retaliated to protect a teammate. "Pat Hickey got high-sticked in the face or the high area or something."

A number of other fights broke out including Beaton taking on Philadelphia center Mel Bridgman.

Game 1, Monday, April 16, 1979
@Philadelphia Flyers 3 Rangers 2 (OT)
Flyers lead series, 1–0

After the Flyers beat the Vancouver Canucks in their preliminary round series, Canucks defenseman Jack McIlhargey (a former Flyer) offered a prediction of their next series with the New York Rangers. "The Rangers won't beat the Philadelphia Flyers because the Flyers are grinders and the Rangers are skaters," said McIlhargey, who added this little caveat, "and anyway, Bobby Clarke will find a way to win."

The best-of-seven matchup featured some juicy storylines including Rangers coach Fred Shero going up against the team he won two Stanley Cups with. The Rangers' compensation to Philadelphia for securing Shero's services came in the form of a 1978 first-round draft choice that the Flyers turned into center Ken "The Rat" Linseman, who would go on to taunt the Rangers for years to come including Game 1 of this playoff series.

Linseman burned the Rangers by scoring the game-winning goal just 44 seconds into overtime to give the Flyers a 3–2 win at the Spectrum. The goal capped off a Flyers comeback from two goals down.

Don Maloney opened the scoring and Phil Esposito's power play goal, his third of the playoffs, gave the Rangers a 2–0 lead midway through the first period. The Flyers got one back when Bob Kelly scored on the power play and it remained 2–1 through a scoreless second period.

The Flyers tied it up with less than five minutes remaining in the third period. Linseman's pass deflected off Carol Vadnais's stick and caromed to Bill Barber, who was stationed on the left side of the Ranger net. Barber put it past John Davidson and the game headed to overtime.

Linseman used his blazing speed to set up the winning score. The 20-year-old rookie intercepted a pass from Vadnais at center ice, brought the puck into the Ranger zone, and cut across the ice to fire the puck past Davidson, who was screened by two Flyers. Philadelphia rookie goaltender Robbie Moore made 22 saves.

The Rangers had the early momentum but could not sustain it as Philadelphia rallied, something the Blueshirts lamented after the loss. "We should have known better against Philadelphia," Vadnais said.

Game 2, Wednesday, April 18, 1979
Rangers 7 @ Philadelphia Flyers 1
Series tied, 1–1

Whatever adjustments that Fred Shero made between Games 1 and 2 must have worked because the Blueshirts went on to rout the Flyers, 7–1, to even the series at a game apiece.

One of those adjustments was promoting Bobby Sheehan, who proved to be a key addition, from the minors. The diminutive (5-foot-7) 30-year-old center was thriving for the New Haven Nighthawks with 33 goals and 81 points and his speed was sorely needed. There was some thought that Ron Duguay should be moved out of center and onto the wing and that Sheehan could provide an answer for Linseman.

Before the game, Sheehan was given his marching orders. "They [Ranger coaches] said 'You're the cat, you gotta take care of the rat,'" Sheehan said recently.

The turning point of the game came late in the first period.

With the game tied, 1–1, and Sheehan in the penalty box, Ron Greschner scored a short-handed goal to give the Rangers a 2–1 lead.

Flyers center Bobby Clarke tried a drop pass that was poked away near center ice by Greschner, who was off to the races. "I just took a swipe at it," Greschner said. "As soon as I poked it off Clarke's stick I was headed toward the net." He skated in all alone and made a move before he flipped the puck past Robbie Moore.

Unlike Game 1, the Rangers took the cue and took control of the game with three goals in the second period to extend the lead to 5–1. Don Maloney's second goal of the playoffs, Greschner's second of the game on the power play, and a goal from Eddie Johnstone, who had five during the season, blew the game open.

Seven minutes into the period, and trailing 4–1, Moore suffered a twisted knee and was replaced by Wayne Stephenson. The Flyers' backup goalie gave up Johnstone's goal and then two more in the third period as Don Murdoch notched his first of the playoffs and Mike McEwen completed the rout with his second of the postseason.

John Davidson stopped 32 shots and gave up just one goal for the third time in his last four games, making some key saves while the game was still close. Flyers right wing Paul Holmgren was stopped by Davidson on a two-on-one with the score tied in the first period. With the Rangers leading, 3–1, in the second period, Reggie Leach's breakaway chance was denied by Davidson.

Greschner, who missed 19 games after he took a hard hit from Buffalo Sabres winger Dave Schultz (a former Flyer) that knocked him out of a game back in February, was starting to get his game back.

It was an impressive rebound by the Rangers from a tough overtime loss in the series opener. Captain Dave Maloney was defiant after the game. "We played a game the way it should be played," he said.

Pat Hickey gave partial credit for the win to Dave Farrish for something that happened during Kate Smith's recording of "God Bless America" that the Flyers played before games for good luck.

"It was the beginning of when they started to turn the lights out in the building for the national anthem," Hickey said. "So it starts up, the technology wasn't there so they have to turn the lights back on for a minute, right? The first stanza that goes through, you sort of hear a click, the lights kinda clicked, and the fans are just about to roar and get into Kate's ending and Davey hears the click and he thinks it's over and he starts [skating] around the net. We started skating around the net and there's a few, 'Boo, what's that guy doing, boo,' so by that time, he ends up coming by our bench and "Shee-cat" [Sheehan] says, 'Keep going,' then everybody else started yelling, 'Keep going, keep going' so Farrish kept going and I'm not sure, but I think Pierre Plante joined him, and by the time he comes around the second time, the crowd is all booing, they're not cheering and there's no frenzy in the building and we won. I always credit Dave Farrish for that win."

Dave Farrish erased Kate Smith's home-ice advantage.
([Public domain photo via Wikimedia Commons)

The Rangers took away Philadelphia's home-ice advantage with a split in the first two games but now they knew they had to hold serve at home beginning with Game 3. Don Murdoch's comment reflected the mindset of a Rangers team that knew they had not won anything yet. "Whether we beat 'em 2–1 or 7–1 it's still one game and I guarantee the Flyers will be ready for the third game," he said.

Sheehan did not get on the scoresheet in his first game with the Rangers but he provided a spark. Murdoch said the diminutive center played bigger than his size. "All of a sudden we're getting ready for Game 2 and here's this little guy comes into the dressing room, I didn't really know much about him. He just went out there and stuck it to Linseman and just controlled them."

Mario Marois felt Sheehan had the right stuff to stymie the

Flyers. "We knew him before," Marois said. "We knew what he was bringing, he was bringing speed."

He also brought some levity according to Nick Fotiu. "He was playing for Nova Scotia Voyagers in Montreal and Al McNeil was his coach. Sheehan has a girl in his room and McNeil knocked on the door and said 'Sheehan, I know you have a girl, you're fined a hundred bucks.' So Bobby opened the door and said, 'Here's a hundred dollars for tonight and another hundred dollars for tomorrow night. Just a really funny guy."

Game 3, Friday, April 20, 1979
Rangers 5 Philadelphia Flyers 1 @ MSG
Rangers lead series, 2–1

Don Maloney scored two goals in a 26-second span of the second period as the Rangers beat the Flyers, 5–1, in Game 3 of their quarterfinal series at Madison Square Garden. The win gave the Rangers a 2–1 lead in the series and snapped their ten-game winless streak at the Garden against Philadelphia.

The Flyers resorted to an old successful formula to be physical with the Rangers during a penalty-filled first period. A total of 52 penalty minutes was handed out by referee Dave Newell, including a five-minute major to Anders Hedberg for fighting with Flyers goaltender Wayne Stephenson, but the tactic worked as Philadephia held a 1–0 lead after one period. That would be the only goal allowed by John Davidson, who made 32 saves

The rookie Maloney's first goal came on a redirection of a Carol Vadnais shot with Flyers defenseman Frank Bathe wrapped all over him. Twenty-six seconds later, Maloney backhanded a shot past Stephenson (who was starting for the injured Robbie Moore) as the Rangers took the lead for good.

Hedberg got some payback with a short-handed goal, his first of the playoffs, that gave the Rangers a 3–1 lead after two periods. In the third period, Ron Duguay scored his first goal of the playoffs and Murdoch netted an empty-netter to close out the scoring.

Special teams continued to be key for the Rangers, who killed off five penalties and have held the Flyers to 2-for-11 with the man advantage so far in the series.

Game 4, Sunday, April 22, 1979
Rangers 6 Philadelphia Flyers 0 @ MSG
Rangers lead series, 3–1

John Davidson was brilliant in net as he recorded his first career playoff shutout in leading the Rangers to a 6–0 whitewashing of the Philadelphia Flyers at the Garden. The win gave the Rangers a stunning three-games-to-one lead in the series with a chance to close it out in Philadelphia in Game 5.

Davidson was particularly sharp in the first period when the Flyers put 14 shots on net. Philadelphia hit two posts and had a goal waved off when the game was already out of hand, but it was Davidson's show, although he wouldn't take all the credit. "This wasn't a John Davidson shutout, it was a Ranger shutout," he said after the game.

With Davidson holding off the Flyers, the Rangers were able to penetrate Flyers goaltender Robbie Moore, who returned to the lineup after being injured in Game 2. The Rangers were outshot, 14–8, but still had a 2–0 lead after one period on goals from Don Murdoch and Eddie Johnstone.

Thanks to Davidson, the Flyers were demoralized and could

never recover. "J.D.," as the crowd chanted, made nine more saves in the second period and the Rangers extended their lead to 4–0. Phil Esposito scored his fourth goal of the playoffs and the newest addition, Bobby Sheehan, scored his first.

The little center provided an unexpected spark that made the Rangers a better team. According to Davidson, when Sheehan joined the team, the Rangers took their game to another level. "All of a sudden, here's this guy and my lord, did he add a different dimension to our team and we just took off."

Murdoch and Johnstone again combined for a pair of goals in the third period. Johnstone's short-handed goal closed the scoring. At that point, Rangers fans began a rendition of "God Bless America," the Kate Smith song that was regarded as the Flyers' good luck charm and was played before home games during their Stanley Cup runs in 1974 and 1975.

At 5-foot-9, Johnstone was playing bigger than his size. "My size is against me, always has been but there's room for the little guy in this game," Johnston said after the game.

The Rangers were outplaying the Flyers in every facet of the game. Even when Philadelphia invoked their physical brand of hockey, the Rangers were capitalizing on the resulting power play chances as they outscored the Flyers with the man advantage, 5–1, during the first four contests.

In two days, they would go for the kill in Game 5 in Philadelphia. Ron Duguay reflected the mindset of the room when he said, "If we keep playing this way and J.D. stays hot, we should win in Philadelphia too."

Game 5, Tuesday, April 24, 1979
Rangers 8 @ Philadelphia Flyers 3

Rangers win series, 4–1

Not even Kate Smith could deny the Rangers a most satisfying and historic victory.

John Davidson continued his outstanding play in net and the Rangers poured it on as they eliminated the Philadelphia Flyers with a memorable 8–3 victory at the Spectrum. The Rangers won four straight after losing Game 1 while outscoring the Flyers, 26–5, in the process.

The Flyers again dusted off Kate Smith's recording of "God Bless America" before the game but the magic ran out as the Rangers completed a 4–1 series victory.

Davidson was sharp early as he continued to frustrate the Flyers and the Rangers slowly began to take control of the game. Midway through the first period, the Rangers took the lead with their sixth power play goal of the series.

Ron Greschner took a pass from Phil Esposito in the high slot and fired the puck through a screen to beat Wayne Stephenson.

Later in the period, the Blueshirts tied an NHL playoff record with their fourth short-handed goal of the series. Walt Tkaczuk broke in on a two-on-one with Anders Hedberg and fired a shot that found the back of the net for a 2–0 lead.

The teams skated through a scoreless second period, so the Rangers were 20 minutes away from advancing to the semifinal against the hated New York Islanders. First, they would close the series with a record-setting third period.

The Rangers took a 5–0 lead period on goals by Walt Tkaczuk, Steve Vickers, and Ron Duguay, but the Flyers did not quit as they answered with three of their own in less than five and half minutes to cut the lead to 5–3.

With a little over three minutes left, the Flyers pulled goaltender Wayne Stephenson, but Carol Vadnais and Eddie Johnstone took advantage with empty-net goals to make it a four-goal advantage. With 34 seconds remaining and Stephenson back in net, Anders Hedberg closed out the scoring. The combined nine goals set the playoff record for a single period. (The mark was tied by the Los Angeles Kings and Calgary Flames in the second period of their game on April 10, 1990. Los Angeles won, 12–4.)

When the final buzzer sounded, the Rangers jumped off the bench to mob John Davidson and they were headed to an epic showdown for a berth in the Stanley Cup Finals.

Davidson was elated with the win but knew the task at hand. "The Islanders are an aggressive team. They show you a little bit of everything and it should be an excellent series."

The addition of Sheehan was arguably the turning point of the series.

Vickers recognized what Sheehan brought to the team for this series against Philadelphia. "He [was a spark, no question about that and they had that guy Linseman, he gave them a little speed there. He kinda offset Linseman in speed and production," Vickers said recently.

The Rangers take care of the Broad Street Bullies in five games to move on.
(Photo courtesy of Pat Hickey)

CHAPTER 14
SEMIFINAL: THE BATTLE FOR NEW YORK

The "Battle for New York" started on April 26, 1979, but the hype really began two days earlier when the Rangers eliminated the Philadelphia Flyers in five games in the quarterfinal. Two days prior to that, the Islanders had taken out the Chicago Black Hawks in a four-game sweep. According to Islanders center Bryan Trottier, they knew all along that the Rangers would be standing in their way to a berth in the Stanley Cup Finals. "We figured we were gonna be playing the Rangers anyway," he said.

For the next few weeks, hockey would become the number one sport in New York. There was a real buzz in the city, one that was supported by extended media coverage. Mario Marois said, "The Garden was crazy at the time. We didn't like the Islanders and they probably didn't like us either."

The Rangers came into the series as heavy underdogs. After all, the Islanders had 116 points, the most in the NHL during the regular season (the first President's Trophy wasn't awarded until 1986) and the Rangers finished twenty-five points behind. Don Murdoch said the Rangers believed all along that they could beat the Islanders in a seven-game series. "There wasn't anybody in our dressing room who thought we could not beat the Islanders," he said. "Playing the Islanders, the adrenaline and the excitement is because we did not like each other."

Walt Tkaczuk said the Rangers had a small window of opportunity to knock off a team that was heavily favored and would eventually cement their legacy with four consecutive Stanley Cups. "We knew the Islanders were a really good team and if we weren't going to beat them that year, that we were probably not gonna beat 'em for a few years, so beating them was going to be like winning a Stanley Cup for us basically. It was so important for the New York Ranger fans and not for the Islander fans, but to beat them was like one of the highlights because we knew they had so much talent."

There were five players on the Rangers' roster that were a part of the team that lost to the Islanders in the 1975 playoffs, including Ron Greschner, who would admit that the crushing loss was on their minds when they met again four years later. "I remember that like it was yesterday," Greschner said. "I remembered going back out for the overtime, skating around, going back to the bench. I wasn't on the ice, I just taped my stick quick, a couple of wraps around my stick. I didn't put the tape down and they started cheering. I didn't know what happened. At first, I thought a fight broke out or something. When the game was over, it was like a shock to us."

The Islanders were extremely confident as well, but they were wary of playing a team who really had nothing to lose since no one expected them to win. Islanders goaltender Chico Resch said that gave the Rangers an edge coming into the series. "There's an advantage to being the underdog and having nothing to lose, until a point," Resch said.

Trottier stressed the importance of winning the first two games at home because the Islanders didn't want to give the Madison Square Garden fans any motivation for Game 3 with a series tie or, shudder the thought, a two-games-to-none deficit. "We have to win these two games," Trottier said. "They're very important because we need the momentum to go into the Garden."

Game 1, Thursday, April 26, 1979
Rangers 4 @ New York Islanders 1
Rangers lead series, 1–0

The Rangers overcame an early deficit to score four unanswered goals as they stunned the Islanders with a 4–1 win in Game 1 of their semifinal series at Nassau Coliseum. A crowd of 14,995 was on hand to see the Rangers take control of the game late in the first period and they never let up.

The Blueshirts were tested early. Don Murdoch took a charging penalty, but two seconds after the Rangers killed it off, Dave Farrish went into the box for slashing. They successfully killed off the second penalty and even though the Islanders would eventually score the game's first goal, defenseman Denis Potvin would rue the missed opportunity after the game. "That killed us," he said. "If we'd have scored early, we would have been all right."

Midway through the first period, Bryan Trottier fired one past John Davidson's glove side for a 1–0 lead but less than five minutes later, a wide-open Murdoch tied the game on the power play with a shot that banged in off the crossbar after goaltender Chico Resch got a piece of it with his glove.

Less than three minutes after the Rangers tied the game, they took the lead for good. Eddie Johnstone was parked in front of the net, where he put in a rebound of a Carol Vadnais shot from the point to give the Rangers a 2–1 lead.

The Rangers put on a defensive clinic in the second period, holding the Islanders to three shots and keeping them bottled up in their own zone thanks to a tenacious and relentless forechecking.

They took a 3–1 lead on a pretty rush up the ice that began when Bobby Sheehan stole the puck near the Rangers blue line. Sheehan crossed the red line and found Pat Hickey streaking down the right-wing side. After entering the Islanders zone, Hickey dropped a pass for Ron Duguay who fired the puck past Resch for a two-goal advantage.

Sheehan would complete the scoring at 16:34 of the second period with his second goal of the playoffs. Pierre Plante was able to beat right wing Mike Bossy and defenseman Pat Price to the puck in the left corner and feed a wide-open Sheehan, who beat Resch through the five-hole.

The third period was relatively quiet and so was the crowd as the Rangers took a surprising 1–0 lead in the best-of-seven series.

As with the previous series against the Flyers, the underdog role seemed to suit the Rangers just fine. "Everybody is expecting the Islanders to win this series and us to be happy just 'cause we got to the semifinals," said Murdoch, "but we're not finished yet. We want to go right to the Finals."

The Rangers seemed to be more battle-tested and brought more energy than the Islanders, who cruised past Chicago in four games. "Philly definitely prepared us," Murdoch said. Resch admitted their apathetic play may have been a result of what happened in the previous series. "It's been a long time since we played an emotional game," he said. "We have to build up some animosity toward the Rangers."

Steve Vickers was pleased with the win. "I don't know if we can play any better than we did tonight," knowing that it was going to take a lot more to beat this opponent.

"'I don't know if we can play any better than we did tonight."
Photo Courtesy of New York Rangers from the lens of George Kalinsky

Game 2, Saturday, April 28, 1979
@New York Islanders 4 Rangers 3 (OT)
Series tied, 1–1

A memorable postseason game between the rivals came to an end when Denis Potvin scored the game-winning goal in overtime to give the Islanders a 4–3 win to even the series at a game apiece.

The winning goal came moments after the Rangers missed an opportunity to end the game. Phil Esposito broke in on left wing and tried to feed Anders Hedberg, who was being checked in front of the Islander net.

Potvin rushed the puck up to the red line and passed to Mike Kaszycki on left wing. Carol Vadnais, who was checking Kaszycki, inadvertently pokechecked the puck to Potvin, who took the shot from the top of the left circle. Using Vadnais as a screen, Potvin's shot deflected off Vadnais's skate and beat John Davidson through his pads at 8:02 of overtime. After the game, Davidson would not blame his defenseman. "You can't play a deflection," he said.

The game was an exciting affair that featured numerous twists and turns.

Walt Tkaczuk pounced on a rebound in front of Islanders goaltender Billy Smith for a 1–0 lead in the first period. Mike McEwen's shot from the slot bounced off Smith's arm, hit the crossbar, and then landed in front where the Rangers center could poke it in.

Early in the second period, the Islanders tied the game, 1–1. Center Bob Bourne skated into the Rangers zone on right wing and crisscrossed with Wayne Merrick, who was left alone on the switch. Davidson tried to challenge the shooter, but Merrick found the five-hole at 1:37 of the second period.

The Rangers regained the lead on a power play goal by Bobby Sheehan, who took the puck off the right-wing boards and fired it past Smith from the right circle for a 2–1 advantage after two periods.

Sheehan had a breakaway early in the third period, but Smith made a huge stop to deny the Rangers a two-goal lead. The Islanders took advantage of the big save as they tied the game a few minutes later. With the puck deep in the Ranger zone, right wing Bob Nystrom fed defenseman Bob Lorimer at the right point, where he blasted it past Davidson for a 2–2 tie.

Less than three and a half minutes later, a sloppy defensive sequence by the Rangers allowed the Islanders to take their first lead of the game. A flurry in front of Davidson culminated in Nystrom scoring the go-ahead goal as he fought off a check from Mario Marois.

With a little over four minutes left in the third period, Phil Esposito tied the game with his fifth goal of the playoffs. Dave Maloney got the puck to Esposito, who threw it towards the net where Don Maloney played it and passed the puck back to Esposito, who put it past Smith for a 3–3 tie. The game headed to overtime where Potvin scored the game-winner.

Before the game, the Coliseum received a bomb threat. Faceoff was scheduled for just after 1 p.m. and a caller, who claimed they were from the Palestine Liberation Organization, said a bomb would go off between 2 and 3 p.m. Coliseum security, along with uniformed, plainclothes, and mounted police all combined to search the arena but, thankfully, no device was found.

Despite the loss, the Rangers were optimistic about their chances as they headed to Madison Square Garden for games 3 and 4. "We beat 'em in one game, we took 'em to overtime in the next and we're going home," Davidson said.

Game 3, Tuesday, May 1, 1979
Rangers 3 @ New York Islanders 1 @ MSG
Rangers lead series, 2–1

There is an enormous amount of pressure in the Stanley Cup playoffs, but Pat Hickey was literally staring down the barrel of a gun the afternoon of Game 3.

He entered a Manhattan bank while a robbery in progress. Three men were wearing stocking masks and carrying guns. At the time, Hickey was quoted as saying, "I thought they were making a movie at first."

During a recent interview, Hickey explained that he went to the bank after the pregame skate. "Four guys came in, one guy like you see in the classic movies, he jumped the teller's bench there. I'm in line and there's a little old lady in front of me and these guys are giving directions and I'm going, 'Am I gonna have to drop the gloves here, is there something I need to do?' I just remember the lady in front of me and she started to whine and I put my arms around her and I was as scared as she was."

One of the gunmen pointed his weapon right at Hickey and told him to "freeze." Thankfully, Hickey was not hurt. One bystander quipped that the threesome may have been the Islanders' top line (Clark Gillies, Bryan Trottier, and Mike Bossy) that was struggling to produce so far in the series. "After all, they never got off a shot," the jokester said.

Hickey was relieved to have gotten out of that situation alive. "I went back home and I saw the news and I think they caught the guys running around the corner and I'm very relaxed and I feel like I'm gonna have a great game 'cause I'm still here," Hickey said, "and what a great, great blessing that I get to entertain 17,500 people."

Hickey acquitted himself well and the Rangers scored a 3–1 win over the Islanders to take a two-game-to-one lead.

Pat Hickey was happy to be alive to play in Game 3.
(Photo courtesy of Pat Hickey)

Despite the Game 2 overtime loss, it was becoming apparent that the Rangers were the better team as they approached Game 3. The Islanders were heading into the cauldron known as Madison Square Garden and they knew they would be facing a hostile and raucous crowd that sensed something exciting was going on with their beloved Rangers.

If the Islanders wanted to take the crowd out of the game by scoring an early goal, the Rangers blew up those plans as the teams skated through a scoreless first period.

In the second period, the Blueshirts got the first goal of the game thanks to their tenacious forecheck which kept the Islanders on their heels. With the Rangers keeping the Islanders in their own zone, Pat Hickey played the puck behind the net and backhanded a pass that floated untouched towards the left point. Mike McEwen fired a shot that bounced off Chico Resch, hit the left post, and bounded into the crease. Defenseman Gerry Hart failed to clear the loose puck and it came right to a wide-open Bobby Sheehan who put it in the open net.

A mistake by the Rangers in their own zone allowed the Islanders to tie the game later in the second period. Mario Marois attempted to play the puck in front of his net but had trouble handling it. Bob Bourne swooped to steal the puck and then backhanded one past John Davidson to tie the game.

The Rangers regained the lead less than three minutes later. From the side of the Islanders net, Don Maloney backhanded a pass to Phil Esposito who was open in front but the puck was deflected into the air. Espo tried to bunt the puck into the net, but missed. After both teams scrambled to gain possession, the puck found its way to Esposito in front who didn't miss this time as he banged it in for a 2–1 lead that the Rangers took to the locker room.

The score remained that way for most of an anxious third period as the Islanders scratched and clawed to get the tying goal while the Rangers tried to hold them off. Then, with six minutes remaining, Steve Vickers stole a cross-ice pass from Stefan Persson that was intended for Denis Potvin and broke in alone on Resch. The goaltender committed to try and challenge Vickers, who deked him out of position, but the puck went off of his stick as he failed to get a shot on the wide-open net.

However, Vickers was able to retrieve the puck and skate behind the net where he was able to beat Resch (who had gotten back into the crease) with a wraparound goal to give the Rangers a 3–1 lead.

During a recent interview, Vickers described the play. "I was kinda hoping that Persson would shoot it up the middle, kind of expecting him to, thinking he would. So I picked it off and almost messed it up. Hopefully I can skate around a goaltender. Just as I was backhanding it, the puck flipped up, so I picked it up again and went around the net. I got around Chico because I saw him come out of the corner of my eye."

Resch felt the only chance he had to make a stop was to challenge Vickers. "I knew it was gonna be a two-on-none otherwise," he said. Vickers said at the time, "I was lucky to get another chance."

Davidson stopped 16 of 17 shots as the Rangers defense continued to frustrate the Islanders. Mike Bossy, who scored 69 goals during the regular season, failed to register a goal or a point in the first three games, while the Islanders were 0-for-14 on the power play. "A lot of people still aren't believing in us," Davidson said, "but we believe in ourselves."

The heavily-favored Islanders were now behind in the series for the second time but there were no signs of panic from coach Al Arbour. "I'm not worrying yet," the future Hall of Famer said.

It was quite a day for Hickey, who was asked what he told people about his frightful experience when he came back to the Garden for the game. "I just said I was in a bank robbery today."

Game 4, Thursday, May 3, 1979
New York Islanders 3 Rangers 2 (OT) @ MSG
Series tied, 2–2

The Rangers had the momentum and the Islanders were facing adversity heading into Game 4. The Islanders' top line of Clark Gillies, Bryan Trottier, and Mike Bossy had produced a total of one goal in the first three games so they were looking to get going in front of a hostile crowd at the Garden.

"No doubt that line is pressing," coach Al Arbour said, "They've just got to go with the flow and enjoy themselves, but the big line has to get going."

The Islanders' top line had one assist on the night, but it was a big one as Gillies assisted on Bob Nystrom's game-winning goal in overtime as Islanders beat the Rangers, 3–2, to even the series at two games apiece with both of their wins coming in overtime.

For the second straight game, the teams skated through a scoreless first period. The Rangers took a 1–0 lead a little over a minute into the second period. Don Maloney gathered a loose puck at center ice and got behind the Islander defense for a breakaway goal that gave the 17,375 at the Garden an early chance to be raucous.

Their jubilation didn't last long. It took just 35 seconds for the Islanders to tie the score. Mike Kaszycki stole the puck from Don Murdoch and found John Tonelli, who broke in on John Davidson and beat him from close range to tie it up.

Early in the third period, the Islanders grabbed a 2–1 lead on a goal from Billy Harris but the Rangers tied the game less than four minutes later. Phil Esposito sent the puck to Don Maloney on the right side of the Islander net. Maloney's shot deflected off a sliding Stefan Persson and changed direction as it filtered past goaltender Billy Smith's right pad for the tying goal.

Davidson made two huge saves towards the end of third period, so for the second time in the series the game went to overtime.

It only took three minutes and 40 seconds to decide the game with the end coming on a frustrating play for Davidson and the Rangers. When Nystrom scooped up a loose puck just inside the Rangers blue line, the goalie took a huge gamble and left his net to challenge the shooter. Davidson made contract with the puck and popped it up in the air, but he was out of position and had no chance to get back in the net. Nystrom found the loose puck and scored as easy a goal as you can have to send Rangers fans home disappointed. "I looked around and there was nobody coming," Nystrom said after the game. "Then it was just a race between me and Big John."

It was a do-or-die play for Davidson. "Usually the puck will bounce away from both of us," Davidson said. "Geez, this one just landed. I couldn't believe it. I was so far out of it."

The series was tied at two games apiece and the Islanders regained the home ice advantage with the pivotal Game 5 set for

Nassau Coliseum two days later.

Bob Nystrom's overtime goal in Game 4 tied the series.
(Photo courtesy of New York Islanders [Public domain],
via Wikimedia Commons)

Game 5, Saturday, May 5, 1979
  Rangers 4 @Islanders 3
  Rangers lead series, 3–2

Bill Chadwick, the revered Rangers' TV color analyst, couldn't have said it any better with his pregame remarks. "Each team up to now has won two games, and each team has won the game they had to. Tonight, it's the Rangers' turn. They have to win this one." At the time, it was one of the most important games in the history of the Rangers and they played like it.

For the fourth consecutive game in the series, the Rangers opened the scoring. With a little over four and a half minutes remaining in the opening period and the teams skating four on four, the Rangers took a 1–0 lead.

Carol Vadnais fired a shot from outside the left circle that came to a wide-open Ron Duguay on the right side of the net, but his shot hit the post. The puck bounced in front of goaltender Billy Smith, who tried to kick it away with his right pad but missed. Don Maloney was planted at the left post and was able to cash in on the rebound.

Less than a minute later, the Rangers had a power play with a chance to go up by two goals but the Islanders stole the puck and tied the game with a short-handed goal. Bob Lorimer came into the Ranger zone on a two-on-one with Lorne Henning on right wing. Lorimer threw a pass in front of the net that goaltender John Davidson made a save on, but the rebound went in off Henning's leg for the tying goal.

The Rangers took a 2–1 lead in the second period off a scramble in front of the net. Mike McEwen took a shot from the slot that bounded up in the air. Smith took a high, wild swing at the puck but was out of position in the crease and then got distracted by Eddie Johnstone in front. Lucien DeBlois was planted at the right side and he backhanded the loose puck into the net for a one-goal lead which the Rangers took into the third period.

The fireworks of an action-packed third period began with a controversial goal by the Islanders that tied the game, 2–2. Mike Kaszycki fired a shot from just inside the Rangers blue line that deflected off Vadnais and floated towards the Ranger net. "I lost sight of the puck and I waved at it," Davidson said after the game. "I was expecting a fastball and he gave me a changeup." Davidson tried to backhand the puck with his glove but wasn't able to and it hit the post and did not go in the net. However, referee Dave Newell ruled it a good goal.

Ninety seconds after tying it up, the Islanders thought they had scored the go-ahead goal. A shot by Denis Potvin trickled past Davidson and appeared to have crossed the goal line but Newell ruled that he already blown the whistle before the puck went in because he thought it was stuck under Davidson's pads.

Maybe the disallowed goal was a sign that this was going to be the Rangers' night. Midway through the period, Ron Greschner gave the Rangers their third lead of the game, beating Smith on the stick side with a wrist shot from the slot. Don Maloney threw the puck towards the slot and it deflected off Phil Esposito's stick right to Greschner, who put it into the net for a 3–2 lead.

The home team came right back and tied the game just 29 seconds later. Bob Bourne took a pass in the slot and beat two Ranger defenders before passing to Bob Nystrom, who was alone in front of the net. Nystrom beat Davidson to set up a frantic final 10 minutes.

Both goaltenders came up with big saves to preserve the tie. Smith denied Anders Hedberg on a breakaway and saved a rebound from going in while Davidson came far out of the crease to challenge Clark Gillies, who had slipped behind the Rangers defense, to make a big save while he submarined the big Islanders left wing.

As time wound down in the third period, it appeared the game was headed to overtime. Both Islanders victories in the series had come in overtime and the Rangers were 8–0 in regulation but 0–3 in overtime during the playoffs.

With less than three minutes left, the Rangers created their chance to win the game. Greschner fired a shot wide of the net that caromed into the right corner. Steve Vickers got to the puck and passed to a cutting Walt Tkaczuk, whose shot was stopped by

Smith. The puck rebounded to the left where Hedberg tried to stuff it in. Smith went down to make the first save but Hedberg was persistent and would not be denied as his second try went in the back of the net to give the Rangers a 4–3 lead that stunned the 14,995 fans at Nassau Coliseum. After he scored the goal, Hedberg hoped he had scored the game-winner. "I do not want to play another overtime," he said.

Davidson snuffed out Nystrom's attempt to tie the game in the final minute and the Rangers had one of the most important victories in franchise history. "We could have mentally died at least three times," Davidson said after the game, "but 20 guys showed guts. Incredible."

When the telecast was over, Chadwick spoke for Rangers fans everywhere when he said, "this crowd here at the Nassau Coliseum CANNOT believe it!!!"

Game 6, Tuesday, May 8, 1979
Rangers 2 Islanders 1 @ MSG
Rangers win series, 4–2

It was the hottest ticket in town and the scalpers were out in force. "Who needs tickets, who wants tickets" was the phrase being bandied about in the area of Madison Square Garden hours before the Rangers, leading the semifinal series three games to two, would take their shot at gaining a berth in the Stanley Cup Finals.

Diehard Blueshirts fans were smelling an elimination game for the hated Islanders. Tickets were reportedly being sold for more than ten times the original price but, to the delight of the scalpers, supply and demand was in order for the fans who desperately wanted to be in the building.

There was a palpable buzz among the fans who arrived early and that only increased when the teams took the ice for the warm-ups. A chant of "Let's Go Rangers" provided a soundtrack as fans and players alike were anxious to get started.

Backup goaltender Doug Soetaert said the Garden was absolutely crazy before the start of Game 6. "It was amazing," Soetaert said recently. "The second the lights would go out, all the people throw fish on the ice. They'd turn the lights on and there'd be 10, 15 fish layin' on the ice in the Islanders zone. They'd be throwing dead fish."

Soetaert said the Islanders were worried about getting hit by them. "I think Billy Smith would be tucked in the net and then all the players, they would start on the blue line and sneak towards the boards and stand right next to the glass because all the people were throwing fish."

After the Rangers failed to capitalize on their first power play of the game, the Islanders snapped an 0-for-19 series streak with the man advantage. Don Murdoch was in the penalty box when the Islanders took a 1–0 lead as Mike Bossy finally got on the scoreboard.

The Rangers failed on a clearing attempt as Denis Potvin gathered the puck near the blue line. Potvin made a cross-ice pass to Stefan Persson, who fired a shot from the point. Bryan Trottier attempted a deflection from the right side of the net, but John Davidson made the save. However, the rebound came out to a wide-open Bossy on the left and he did not miss.

The Islanders landed the early blow and led 1–0 after one period. In the locker room between periods, Davidson said the Rangers were down but not out. "There was kind of a leery feeling in here after the first period," said Davidson, "but in the second, everyone went out and did this own job, and we just turned it around."

A little over five minutes into the period, Mario Marois fired a shot from the right point. Chico Resch made the save but the rebound came to a wide-open Don Murdoch on the left side. Resch was down and Murdoch took his time, as he spun around for a forehand shot that beat the goaltender to tie the game.

A few minutes later, the Rangers went on the power play and took the lead for good. With Bob Lorimer in the penalty box, the Rangers cashed in on the opportunity for a 2–1 lead. Ron Greschner fired a shot from between the faceoff circles, just inside the blue line. Phil Esposito screened Resch and the puck found the back of the net as the Garden crowd erupted.

Esposito was originally credited with the goal, but during a succeeding stoppage in play, he made it a point to let the official scorer know that it was Greschner's goal and not his. "He [Greschner] deserved it," Esposito said after the game.

The Rangers still led by a goal after two periods and were 20 minutes away from going to the Stanley Cup Finals for the first time in seven seasons. Pat Hickey said, "After the second period, we looked around at each other and said, 'Hey, it's here. Let's take it.' We realized we really could do it."

The third period was a textbook display of how to protect a lead as the Rangers were all over the puck, did not give the Islanders much room to operate, and held them to three shots for the entire period, as chants of "J.D., J.D." rained down from the crowd. "It's by far the easiest third period I've had in the playoffs," Davidson said. In the series, the Rangers held the dynamic Islanders' power play to one goal in twenty attempts.

When the clock struck zero, Davidson raised his arms in triumph and Potvin struck an iconic pose as he lay on the ice, propped up against the sideboards, looking exhausted from the battle. "It went so well for us for eight months," Potvin said, "and then, bang, it turned around in two weeks." Bossy credited the Rangers for taking it to them. "The truth is that the Rangers stood up to us and played us out."

Thousands of delirious fans poured out onto the streets yelling "We're number one" and "Stanley Cup Rangers." At the 33rd Street entrance where the visiting team's bus pulled out, a large gathering of fans were chanting, "Goodbye Islanders, we hate to see you go."

It was a great victory for the Rangers but there was still the ultimate goal of ending their 39-year drought without a Stanley Cup championship. Esposito, who already had his name engraved on the coveted chalice twice, said there's more work to be done. "We'll be greedy," Esposito said. "We won't be satisfied with this."

Keeping the Islanders' top line of Gillies, Trottier, and Bossy in check was one of the keys to the Rangers' win. Tkaczuk felt they matched up very well with the talented trio. "If you look at that line, you had a great center man in Trottier who could make plays and everything else, a Bossy who could score goals. We countered that with Anders Hedberg, a goalscorer," Tkaczuk said recently. "Then you had Clark Gillies, a big, strong guy, and we had "Sarge" Vickers, also a strong guy, but he's not a fighter, but a strong guy who could score goals. Fred [Shero] wanted to put, probably, a good, solid defensive as well as offensive line against that line because that's the way they played. He thought our line gave him that and we held our own against one of the best lines in hockey."

Hedberg's line held it's own against the Isles' big three.
(Photo by Mark Rosenman)

Davidson recently reflected on beating the Islanders. "That series, to me, I think we won because I think we showed resiliency.

He was blunt in saying they caught the Islanders at the right time, just before they began their four-year run as Stanley Cup champs. "They had to find a way to learn how to win. They did a masterful job."

Davidson said he sees former Islanders and Hall of Famers Billy Smith and Denis Potvin and they swap stories from the 1979 playoffs. "We sit and talk and we say hello to each other. A great deal of respect for each other. We turned the city on. We turned a great big area right onto hockey and put it right up there with anything else, the two teams."

Doug Soetaert remembered sitting in the Felt Forum theater at the Garden as the Islanders were leaving the building. "Their bus would leave from underneath there and the fans were throwing stuff at their bus and abusing them as they left," he said. "It was a crazy time. It was a good crazy because everybody was excited.

You know what I mean? Yeah, it was a crazy time in the sense that it was exciting and the whole city was just rocking at the time."

Pat Hickey harkened back to when the series ended as he said recently, "I remember thinking at the time that these guys are going to be really pissed off next year."

CHAPTER 15
STANLEY CUP FINALS: COMING UP SHORT

After beating the Islanders in six games in the semifinal, the Rangers had to wait to see who their opponent would be in the Stanley Cup Finals. Two days after the Rangers' stunning victory, the three-time defending Stanley Cup champion Montreal Canadiens ended a thrilling seven-game semifinal against the Boston Bruins with a 5–4 victory on Yvon Lambert's overtime goal.

The Canadiens were shooting for a fourth consecutive Cup while the Rangers were trying to snap a 39-year drought.

In beating the Islanders, the Rangers eliminated the team that led the NHL with 116 points. Montreal was second with 115, but the Rangers were not intimidated by them. They had beaten the Canadiens three times in four meetings during the regular season, including both games in Montreal, so their confidence level was high heading into the Finals. Phil Esposito, who had won two Stanley Cups with the Boston Bruins, said the Rangers got their act together at the right time to get to this point. "This team just sort of grew together during the course of the season and peaked during the playoffs."

Game 1, Sunday, May 13, 1979
Rangers 4 @Canadiens 1
Rangers lead series, 1–0

The Rangers couldn't have asked for a better result in Game 1 of the Final at the Montreal Forum as they scored a 4–1 victory over the Canadiens to take a 1–0 lead in the series.

John Davidson continued his brilliant play as he stopped 31 of 32 shots while the Rangers' special teams were a huge factor in the win. The Blueshirts scored two power play goals and a short-handed goal, while Montreal went 0-for-6 on the power play.

On the Rangers' first power play of the game, Steve Vickers had an easy tip-in goal that was the result of Anders Hedberg's pass through the crease, giving them a 1–0 lead. Ron Greschner's unassisted goal late in the period gave the Rangers a 2–0 lead at the end of the first period.

Even though they had the lead, the Rangers were still tight. Guy Lafleur cut their lead in half when he scored at 7:07 of the second period but a little less than two and half minutes later, Phil Esposito scored his seventh of the playoffs on the power play to make it a two-goal lead. It was Espo's 56th career playoff goal.

Dave Maloney's short-handed goal late in the second put the game away. Maloney was the trailer on a rush up the ice. He took a drop pass from Hedberg and put a wrist shot past Montreal goaltender, future Hall of Famer, Ken Dryden, for a three-goal advantage. "Maloney outraced all of our forwards," Canadiens coach Bowman said after the game. "None of our forwards skated with him. He made it a 3-on-2 play instead of a 2-on-2."

The final Ranger goal by Maloney was also Dryden's undoing as he was lifted for the first time ever in a playoff game. Backup goalie Michel "Bunny" Larocque replaced him for the third period and received raucous cheers from the hometown fans when he was introduced.

Dryden and Larry Robinson, one of three future Hall of Fame defensemen on the Montreal team (Guy Lapointe and Serge Savard the others), were not the only culprits in the loss but they felt the wrath of the Forum fans as they were lustily booed. Robinson twice failed to clear the puck out of his own zone and both times the Rangers recovered the puck and scored a goal.

"Every time we made a mistake it was in their net," said Robinson. Lapointe was missing from Montreal's lineup and it showed as Robinson and Savard had to log an inordinate amount of ice time. The Rangers were able to wear them down and take advantage of their fatigue. "We did the same thing to [Islanders defenseman Denis] Potvin," Pierre Plante said.

Following the win, the Rangers were 3–0 at the Forum, a notoriously tough place to win, especially in postseason. Ron Duguay did not get on the scoresheet, but it wasn't because he was intimidated by playing in Montreal. "I was a little nervous before the game but then we went out for warm-ups," Duguay said. "I looked at them and I looked at us. Those guys aren't better than we are."

Ulf Nilsson returned to the lineup for the first time since breaking his ankle against the Islanders in late February but did not get much ice time.

Larocque had beaten the Rangers, 1–0, at Madison Square Garden in late March for their only win against the Rangers during the regular season so Bowman would have a decision to make for Game 2. The Rangers had no such decision to make as they were riding on the back of Davidson during this remarkable playoff run that would eventually come to a screeching halt.

Game 2, Tuesday, May 15, 1979
@Canadiens 6 Rangers 2
Series tied, 1–1

The Rangers were feeling very good about themselves after their Game 1 win and they carried that over into Game 2, but things went south and Montreal scored six unanswered goals to even the Finals at a game apiece with a 6–2 win.

After Ken Dryden was lifted in the series opener, the assumption was Scotty Bowman would start Michel Larocque in net. That was the original plan, but things changed during the pregame warm-ups when Larocque took a Doug Risebrough shot off the top part of his mask that caused him to fall to the ice. The shot broke Larocque's mask and he was taken to the hospital for observation. Dryden returned as the starter and after a shaky start, he settled down and stopped the Rangers' last 22 shots.

Anders Hedberg beat Dryden on the first shot of the game as he put a 35-foot wrister past the Montreal netminder just 1:02 into the game. Duguay scored on the Rangers' third shot for a 2–0 lead at 6:21 of the first. Boos rained down on Dryden from the Montreal faithful but even with the two-goal lead, Hedberg felt the Rangers were getting outplayed. "They [Montreal] were controlling the game, even at that point," he said.

In what seemed like an instant, the Canadiens stormed back to grab a 3–2 lead. Yvon Lambert's leg redirected Mario Tremblay's shot past John Davidson to cut the deficit, then Guy Lafleur backhanded a rebound into the net for his 10th playoff goal and a 2–2 tie.

A little over four minutes later, Davidson gave up a bad goal to allow Montreal to take a one-goal lead. Future Hall of Famer Bob Gainey's 35-foot shot hit Davidson's stick, but he couldn't corral the puck and it went in the net for a crushing goal.

Goals by two more future Hall of Famers gave the Canadiens a 5–2 lead in the second period. Steve Shutt picked Phil Esposito's pocket to score an unassisted goal and Jacques Lemaire's power play goal tally gave the Canadiens a three-goal lead. Mark Napier scored off an odd-man rush to close out the scoring in the third period.

The Rangers may have felt like they let one get away, but they were simply outplayed. "No team in the world could've beaten them tonight," Dave Maloney said afterwards. Coach Fred Shero got straight to the point when he said, "Nothing was wrong, they just played very well. We couldn't do much about it."

Game 3, Thursday, May 17, 1979
Montreal Canadiens 4 Rangers 1 @ MSG
Canadiens lead series, 2–1

Billy Joel sang the national anthem and the crowd at Madison Square Garden was fired up for Game 3 of the Stanley Cup Finals, but it quickly turned into a disappointing evening as the Canadiens took a 2–1 series lead with a 4–1 win.

The Rangers were hoping that the fans' unmatched passion would give the team an edge. During a recent radio interview, Ron Greschner reflected on the electric atmosphere that engulfed the historic building. "The Garden is just like, electrifying," Greschner said. "The fans are without a doubt, they're the best fans of any kind, football, basketball, baseball, I don't care what fan you're gonna pick, the Ranger fans are the best fans you can probably imagine, and they know the game. It was the best year in hockey that I had."

Montreal scored on its first shot of the game and never looked back. Steve Shutt took advantage of an opening in front of the net to score on the power play at 7:27 of the first period for a 1–0 lead. With a little over four minutes left in the first period, Doug Risebrough completed a three-on-two rush with a shot from the left faceoff circle that beat John Davidson and Montreal extended their advantage to 2–0.

The Rangers were being thoroughly outplayed but they hung in during a scoreless second period and were down by only two goals entering the third period.

At 6:06 of the third, the Garden crowd came to life when Ron Duguay cut the Canadiens' lead in half with his fifth goal of the playoffs. He won a faceoff in the offensive zone and fired a wrist shot that appeared to be going wide of the net but deflected off Serge Savard's skate and eluded Ken Dryden.

Less than nine minutes later, Montreal got the goal that broke the Rangers' backs as they also capitalized on a deflection. Yvon Lambert shot the puck towards the net and Mario Tremblay skated in front and the puck deflected in off his skate for a 3–1 lead. With less than three minutes remaining in the third period, the Rangers got caught in the offensive zone and Jacques Lemaire capped off a three-on-one break with his eighth goal (with a secondary assist from Dryden) of the playoffs to put the game away.

The Canadiens regained home-ice advantage and the Rangers' momentum from their win in Game 1 seemed to have dissipated. "In the last couple of games, we lost the momentum that we had," Walt Tkaczuk said. "We are handling the puck like a hot potato. We are being outworked and out hustled."

The Blueshirts were down but not out according to captain

Dave Maloney. "I don't think there's any cause to jump off the Brooklyn Bridge as a group just because we're down 2–1. We've just got to regroup, look ahead, keep our heads up, and be proud."

Game 4, Saturday, May 19, 1979
Montreal Canadiens 4 Rangers 3 (OT) @ MSG
Canadiens lead series, 3–1

Serge Savard put a backhander past John Davidson at 7:25 of overtime to give the Canadiens a 4–3 win and a 3–1 lead in the Stanley Cup Finals.

There was a bizarre set of circumstances that preceded the winning goal. Larry Robinson fired a slap shot that appeared to beat Davidson and hit the back of the net, but the red light never went on and play continued.

When the whistle blew a few minutes later, Montreal argued the call but to no avail. It became a moot point when Savard scored a few moments later.

Pat Hickey gave the Rangers a 1–0 lead in the first period when he fired the puck towards the crease and it deflected off the back leg of Ken Dryden into the net. One minute and twenty seconds later, Montreal tied the game. Rejean Houle took advantage of an open net when Davidson left his post and misplayed the puck to score his first goal of the playoffs

Pat Hickey gave the Rangers a short-lived 1-0 lead.
(Photo courtesy of Pat Hickey)

Don Murdoch's seventh playoff goal gave the Rangers a 2-1 lead after one period but Montreal dominated the second period, outshooting the Rangers, 16-4, tying the game on a goal from Yvon Lambert.

The Rangers took their third lead of the game in the third period. Phil Esposito scored his eighth goal of the playoffs for a 3-2 lead but Montreal tied the game a little over two minutes later on a goal by Bob Gainey to send the game to overtime.

Davidson said that Gainey's tying goal was one that he wished he had back. "Puck came out of the corner, to him [Gainey] in kind of a semi-slot and he fired a quick wrist shot to beat me. To this day, I questioned myself for not going into the butterfly [by dropping to his knees]. I stood up and it didn't cover enough net because it was a low shot. If I would've gone in the butterfly, it [the puck] would've hit my left pad and it still bugs me."

Steve Vickers lamented the overtime loss that really took the air out of the Rangers' balloon. "Montreal outplayed us in overtime," Vickers said. "They [Montreal] had a great hockey club."

Game 5, Monday, May 21, 1979
@Montreal Canadiens 4 Rangers 1
Canadiens win series, 4–1

The Rangers' fun postseason ride finally came to a screeching halt.

The Canadiens thoroughly dominated Game 5 of the Finals, 4–1, to capture their fourth consecutive Stanley Cup. The loss meant that the Rangers would extend their Cup-less drought to 39 years with the usual lament from the losing team, "Wait till next year." Little did anyone know at the time, that it would be another 15 years before the streak would end.

Rangers coach Fred Shero had no answers for a Montreal team that was flying for 60 minutes as they put 31 shots on John Davidson. The gallant netminder was playing with a swollen knee as the result of a ligament injury that he suffered in the final game of the semifinal series against the Islanders. Davidson kept quiet about the injury as he didn't want to have an excuse, but it clearly hampered his play.

Davidson was screened when Montreal's Rich Chartraw opened the scoring midway through the first period. With a little over three minutes left in the period, the Rangers appeared to gain some momentum when Carol Vadnais deflected a Don Murdoch shot past Ken Dryden. The first period ended with the teams tied but Dave Maloney took a penalty with one second remaining that was a portent of things to come.

Montreal took advantage of the power play opportunity and overwhelmed the Rangers in the second period as they broke open the game with three goals. "They gave us a lesson in good ol' fashioned hockey," Steve Vickers said after the game.

Just over a minute into the first period, Montreal's Jacques Lemaire rushed the puck up the ice and fired a shot just outside the blue line that beat Davidson for a power play goal and a 2–1 lead. It was the one goal that he had second thoughts about because it came from outside the blue line and it's one that he usually handled. Goals by Rejean Houle and Jacques Lemaire rounded out the scoring.

In the end, the Rangers were outmatched by a dynasty.

One of the unanswered questions surrounding the Finals loss was why Nick Fotiu wasn't in the lineup to provide a much-needed physical presence against Montreal. Fotiu played in the series against the Flyers but did not see a second of ice time the rest of the way.

According to Bobby Sheehan, "Nick's a great hockey player, he's got the muscle and should have someone up there to get some room in the corners and all that. I think Nick would help immensely."

Shero made the decision to sit Fotiu in the last two rounds. Years later, Fotiu and Shero were at a party when the former coach made an admission to his former player. "He said, 'I made two mistakes in my life and one wasn't playing you. I listened to somebody that I shouldn't have listened to and I made two mistakes, one was not playing you.' That's all he said," Fotiu remembered.

CHAPTER 16
EPILOGUE: "WOULDA, COULDA, SHOULDA"

In the aftermath of the loss to Montreal in the Finals that put a bit of a damper on what was a terrific and exciting postseason run, there were many theories floated around as to why the Rangers didn't win.

There's no shame in losing to one of the all-time great teams in NHL history. The 1978–79 Montreal Canadiens won their their fourth consecutive Stanley Cup and sixth in the past nine seasons. Montreal's lineup featured ten Hall of Famers but only nine played in the Final. (Yvan Cournoyer missed most of the season with a back injury but his name was still engraved on the Stanley Cup.)

The Rangers played Montreal so well during the regular season that some felt they had a legitimate shot to upset this great team. The Rangers won their first three games against the Canadiens during the season, two in Montreal, and lost the final meeting at the Garden, 1–0. After winning Game 1 of the Stanley Cup Finals in Montreal, the Rangers had a 2–0 lead in Game 2 but it was all downhill from there.

During a radio interview, Phil Esposito lamented what could've been. "Freddie Shero made a terrible mistake and I said it even when I was playing," he said. "After the first game, we win the first game in Montreal. I went to Freddie Shero because he had taken the captaincy away from me as the oldest guy, and I said, 'Freddie, let's get everybody out of Montreal. This is too good of a town. We could be in trouble. We just won and could win the Cup,' he said, 'Nah, everybody's okay.'

Esposito was a two-time Stanley Cup winner but Shero, a two-time winner himself, failed to heed the warning. "Everybody wasn't okay," Esposito said. "Too many of those young guys and too many of the older guys didn't believe because they never were there before, so they didn't take care of themselves in those two days before the next game."

Ron Duguay agreed with Esposito's assessment. "Phil's probably right because I can remember the first night, and I shouldn't admit this, but our first night, our first game, we beat Montreal in Montreal and I can remember rolling in the next day at six in the morning, which was the wrong thing to do," Duguay said. "It was what we had been doing all year is what we were doing in the playoffs. We didn't change anything, but, at that point, we were tired, physically tired. We needed to pull back, but lot of us didn't."

Bobby Sheehan remembered Esposito speaking to Shero about staying in Montreal. "It's a tough decision but I wouldn't be staying [in] downtown Montreal [for] two or three days," he said. "When the Bruins beat the Canadiens, you know where they stayed? They stayed across the river in New York, Niagara Falls, New York. I don't know if that had anything to do with it, it was just a thought."

Esposito put the blame squarely on Shero. "I never forgave Freddie Shero for that. It was his fault and we could have won a Cup then without a doubt. John Davidson was on top of his game. Never did J.D. play like that before and never would he ever play it again."

Davidson was a bit more appreciative of the experience that

he gained during the Rangers' run to the 1979 Stanley Cup Finals. "It's complicated when you're trying to win in New York, and it's a wonderful thing because if you ever get a chance to pass that test, I'd recommend it to all the players if you have a chance to play in New York, play in New York, at least for a while, and then if you can pass that test, you can pass any tests because it's a demanding way of playing the game from everyone involved. It's fantastic, it toughens you up. It makes you learn how to win, makes you learn how to deal with losses."

It would be 15 more seasons before the Rangers would win another Cup and end a 54-year drought, but this 1978–79 team will always be remembered with fondness and everlasting affection for the exciting and surprising postseason run they gave their diehard fans.

CHAPTER 17
WHERE ARE THEY NOW?

Frank Beaton is retired now. "I just moved to Florida, my son's been living down there, so I moved there because I'm about to be a grandfather for the first time, so I moved down to be closer for that," Beaton said. "Previously I had been living up in Nova Scotia and working up there and of course I still have a place in Birmingham, Alabama where I settled after the Birmingham Bulls [World Hockey Association] days."

John Davidson, who is currently the president of hockey operations for the Columbus Blue Jackets, is also remembered by Rangers fans as a long-time hockey broadcaster. On June 4, 2009, it was announced that Davidson would be honored by the Hockey Hall of Fame with the Foster Hewitt Memorial Award for his contributions to broadcasting. He was also on the call for Madison Square Garden TV when the Rangers captured the 1994 Stanley Cup.

"Sam Rosen [TV Voice of the Rangers] and I felt like we were part of that team for sure. And uh, to see that team get put together and having Mark Messier come in and be the emotional leader for that club along with the talent they had with [Brian] Leetch and [Mike] Richter and [Alexei] Kovalev and they brought in [Steve] Larmer, there's a lot of things there that were, that were really, really good to make that team win," Davidson said. "I also, that season, did a lot of broadcasting throughout the league that were not Ranger games and I knew the Rangers were the best team. They just were. Yet you saw how hard it was to win, to beat the

Devils like they did, that was a battle. To beat Vancouver, that should have been a four-game series. It ended up being seven. The Rangers should very well have won that thing in four games. [Vancouver Canucks goaltender] Kirk Mclean had a couple of games that were out of this world and so boom, next thing you know, it's seven and it's tight. I hope that team doesn't get forgotten. That was a team that came out of nowhere. It was [a] really young [team] that had some good leadership and did something that was out of nowhere and it turned that that city on. Even after we lost, we went home and we were very disappointed. A couple of days later, they invited us down to City Hall and to introduce us, etcetera. We were exhausted, but we did it, and the response, by the people that were there was just, just incredible, and we didn't win. Ninety-four, when the Rangers won, everybody went down to the Canyon of Heroes by God. I've never seen anything like that. That was a million people. All you saw were people's heads and eyes. It was special, it really was. That team [1978–79] was a good group that really, really did something in my opinion that was special but didn't win it all."

Lucien DeBlois said he was semi-retired. "I was a pro scout with the Vancouver Canucks the last 15 years, prior to that with the Ducks of Anaheim. So the last 25, 26 years since I retired from playing I've been in hockey, and so fortunate to be with the NHL teams that I was. Fortunate enough to stay in the game and work a different capacity as a scout for the Canucks, for the Ducks, and some minor league teams also. I just loved it right now, retired from the NHL, but I'm still watching some hockey and I'm doing some consulting for my son who is a player agent in hockey, so I'm still in hockey indirectly."

His fondest memory of that team: "Every time I see Nicky [Fotiu] at the Rangers' golf tournament and "Doogs" [Ron Duguay], Donny Maloney, and Gresh [Ron Greschner] it's just tremendous. All these guys. We had such a great time and great team and even though we didn't, win it all, we did everything in our power to try to, we, such a tremendous friendship and bond that you will always remember!"

Andre Dore went to work in the financial world. "After my hockey career, I worked for a couple of different firms on Wall Street for like 25, 26 years, Bear Stearns being among the best known one," he said. "Then, like five years ago when that gig ran out of steam, I got connected to Integral Hockey (which according to its website, features the most technologically advanced composite hockey stick repairs on the market) by LinkedIn, of all places, with this company. It was posted in a group. I was invited to join, called hockey players doing business together and somehow these guys were on there. So I didn't know anything about it. I contacted the CEO and I thought this was kind of interesting and one thing led to another and that's where I am today."

Ron Duguay became a pre- and postgame studio analyst for Rangers telecasts on MSG Network from 2007 to 2018. In 2009, six years after his retirement from professional hockey, Duguay returned to the ice to play two games in the EPHL for the "Garden of Dreams" charity, a non-profit organization that is associated with Madison Square Garden. Duguay played one game with the Brooklyn Aces and one with the Jersey Rockhoppers.

Phil Esposito was inducted into the Hockey Hall of Fame in 1984. Esposito was the Rangers' general manager and coach in the mid-1980s. He was a driving force in winning the expansion bid for the Tampa Bay Lightning. Esposito also served as team president and GM until 1998 and is currently part of their broadcast team.

Dave Farrish retired from coaching with the Colorado Avalanche in 2017. "I just took a scouting job with the Blues this year as a pro scout covering the West," Farrish said.

Nick Fotiu focused on working with players after his playing career was over. "I was with the San Jose farm team and then I went from San Jose to the Rangers, you know that down in Hartford and through the course of that. developed, you know, 55 players that played in the National Hockey League," Fotiu said. "Guys like Jed Ortmeyer, Steve Valiquette, Jamie Lundmark, Jonathan Cheechoo, Dan Boyle, [Evgeni] Nabokov, [Miikka] Kiprusoff, all of these guys that made it, 55 of them played in National Hockey League that I had developed. I'm very proud of that." Looking back at the 1978–79 team, he says, "Well, my fondest memory of that year is the people, the fans in Madison Square Garden, and how we could have had it and that's why I wanted it."

Ron Greschner heads the Ron Greschner Foundation to support autism research and awareness.

Anders Hedberg is retired from hockey. "I've been in hockey all my life. Very fortunate. I still love the game watching it. I still have some business interests that keep me busy," Hedberg said. "I live just outside of Stockholm where I have a wonderful home with a nice piece of water. Hopefully it will be some ice there in the winter time and I have three kids, four grandchildren. Everybody is healthy, and well educated, and living a terrific life."

Fondest memory: "I have a picture in my fitness room. In the picture I'm on my way. Just jumping off the bench on my way walking beside me is Eddie Johnstone, and we have, the biggest smiles," he said. "We were on our way to J.D. [John Davidson] on the ice, with the team's biggest smiles you can see. On the same picture, I have two Islanders, Denis Potvin and [Mike] Bossy, whose faces are totally different. It's an unbelievable picture that I can see every time I walk into my fitness room, of the difference between a winning face and a losing face and being a Ranger, it's a wonderful picture, wonderful picture. That moment when I'm on my way to celebrate with Davey Maloney and J.D. the win against the Islanders, that is my moment from that season."

Pat Hickey was another player who went into the financial world. "I worked with the largest company in Canada, the Royal Bank of Canada, in the brokerage arm for wealth management, helping people and institutions like healthcare conglomerates," Hickey said. "I managed their money through certain research that goes on. That's what I've done basically is managed money for the last 30, 40 years and building that business and then basically being a salesman. I'm also on the board of the Ranger alumni and I helped start that, with Steve Vickers and Bill Chadwick [former Ranger announcer], then built the Ice Hockey in Harlem program that's like 33 years old now and still running.

Most vivid memory of '79: "Getting out of the bank robbery alive and in time to play Game 3 of the semifinals." (See Chapter 14.)

Eddie Johnstone went into coaching. "I started coaching junior and then I coached in my hometown in Vernon [British Columbia] and I coached junior team there and that's kind of ironic because that's where I started to play," Johnstone said. "In 1992, I coached pro. I was down in the East Coast League; I coached three years in Pennsylvania and then I started a team in the East Coast League in Mobile, Alabama, and then I coached in the American League for a year. I came back home and I coached another junior team 'til about 2004, and in the meantime, I went to work for this construction company and I'm still with them. I've been there for 19 years now."

Most vivid memory: "The people during the Islander-Rangers series. I have never heard people cheer as loud, maybe it was because it was the Islanders and for three quarters of every period it was 'Potvin Sucks,' that chant was about every 30 or 40 seconds it seemed like, but those games are my most vivid memories. Maybe it would be different if things had turned out differently in Montreal. If we won, if J.D. played that series healthy, he was a gamer. He kept plugging away, but for sure it was the six games against the Islanders."

Dave Maloney has been the color analyst alongside Kenny Albert on Rangers radio since the 2005–06 season. He began his broadcast career in 1995 as a studio analyst for Fox NHL Saturday.

Don Maloney retired from the NHL in 1991 and moved into the front office of the New York Islanders in 1992. From 1996 to 2007, he served under Rangers president Glen Sather as the assistant GM and vice president of player personnel. From 2007 to 2016, Maloney was the general manager of the Arizona Coyotes.

Mario Marois: "Well, I was working until last June 18 for the Detroit Red Wings as an amateur scout. I've been a scout for about 18 years now. Looking for a job at the moment. I am a part-time lumberjack. I love being outdoors and cutting firewood. I do all sorts of stuff. I spend a lot of time in a wood shop, I like that. I'm not very good at it. I'm just starting. But I, uh, I enjoy going to that too."

Most vivid memory: "Well, my favorite time was the simple things like the nights before a game. I used to go out with J.D. and he wanted to have a few beers before he went to bed. So we went out and that's probably a favorite moment, you know, it was the big guy who wanted to have a good sleep and a couple of beers and went home early and ready for the next day. Yeah. John Davidson was a good guy to play with. He as well as Ron Greschner were just special teammates. We had so many good guys on that team and they are all part of my good memories of that year."

Mike McEwen: "I played in Switzerland for four years as a player and then an assistant coach in New Haven. I coached the Oklahoma Blazers here [Oklahoma City] from '92 to '95, in the old Central Hockey League for three years. We were the most successful minor-league hockey franchise in the history of minor league hockey at that point. We had 10,400 people for an average, and my winning percentage was like .665. I mean, it was crazy. We had Hooter girls, Miller girls. Bud girls, I mean, I think a lot of those kids came in the building knowing they can drink under age. It was kind of a crazy deal; it was "A" [level] hockey wasn't even AA, it was below the East Coast League, but then I got fired and divorced in the same month. I thought I'd retired from hockey and I sort of took a break for two years, went back to Toronto and I did end up coaching the AA and AAA, assistant coaching, the guy let me run the practices and stuff. In '98, I got involved in youth hockey, at different points in time I've been president of three associations here. Now I run the beginner program, the house rec program. I've done the travel program at different points in the 20 years. I give lessons, I run camps. We have over 360 kids in the hockey program here. Two hundred and sixty in the house league and 100 in our beginner so I'm still on the ice 15, 20 hours a week."

Fondest memory: "I got 20 goals that year. That was pretty special for a defenseman, it was just great to go the rink and great to be around that team every day."

Don Murdoch worked as a scout for the Tampa Bay Lightning under Phil Esposito. In 1998, Murdoch was scouting the Quebec Major Junior Hockey League (QMJHL) where he saw an 18-year old prospect named Brad Richards. According to the *St. Petersburg Times*, Murdoch labeled Richards as the "next [Hall of Famer] Mark Recchi." Richards put together a 15-year NHL career that is Hall of Fame worthy.

Ulf Nilsson is living in Stockholm, retired with a hobby business, self-storage for wine serving about 100 customers in two locations. His greatest memory of that season was being voted the MVP by the players.

Bobby Sheehan: "I've been crying ever since. No, I actually work for the Massachusetts State Lottery as an investigator. I go around to the bingo halls and make sure they don't steal money. I really like what I do. It's a great job on the night shift because no one can find me. I've been here 31 years. If I didn't like it, I get out. I got some help from a Hall of Famer, one of the best Hall of Famers helped me to get the job. So I won't mention any names, but he's from Boston and it's all I can tell you."

Doug Soetaert: "When I retired from playing, I ended up taking a job with the New York Rangers. I ran the Denver, Colorado Rangers at that time, the farm team, and I was an assistant coach, assistant GM for a couple years and then went back to New York, was a pro scout for [Rangers GM] Neil Smith. Then, I came out to Kansas City and spent, I think it was 11 years in Kansas City running the International Hockey League team. Then we got a full affiliation with the San Jose Sharks and then when the IHL and the American Hockey League merged; we ended up not making it into that merger because they had the Grand Rapids team. They were allowed to have one team in the American League. So we ended up closing shop here, I went out to the Western Hockey League, 'Major Juniors' and started up a brand-new franchise out there. I was the general manager from day one and put an organization together and actually went to the Western Hockey League Finals, year one with an expansion team. So I was able to put an expansion team together and ran that for 11 years and then we parted ways and so I went to Europe, worked for Red Bull for two years, one year in the Austrian league and one year in the German league, was doing some pro scouting and helping with player personnel for Don Jackson, who was the head coach in Salzburg, Austria for Red Bull hockey. He hired me to do player development and player recruiting. Then I came back and Donny Maloney hired me to be the pro scout for the Arizona Coyotes. I worked in the minors with the Coyotes and our staff was let go in our last year of our contract so I'm looking for something at the moment."

Most memorable moment: "Well, obviously going to the Finals, you know, that was, pretty special, being part of that organization, I was drafted by the New York Rangers, I still consider myself a Ranger. I haven't been back in a long time, but it was a very exciting time in a great city. I always loved playing there, but that year, even though I didn't play, that was a special, special, special season, for the players, for the fans and for the organization, that's for sure."

Dean Talafous: "Well, I started at the University of Minnesota. Herb Brooks called the University of Minnesota where he coached, and he said Talafous retired and you might want to hire him as an assistant. So I started at the University of Minnesota as an assistant coach. Took the job at UW, University of Wisconsin River Falls, and in five years I won a national championship [and] National Coach of the Year for college. Then I took a job up in Anchorage, Alaska, a Division I job and the WCHA, coached up there five years. Then I came back and I started Total Hockey, which was player development, off-ice total player development for all ages, all abilities with technology and tracking system. I developed that and started that and built 20 of them around North America. A lot of them for ex-NHL guys like Denis Potvin in Florida, different guys. So I was real involved in player development with the franchise business. Then I sold that eight years ago when I was retired for a year and a half and the high school team in Hudson, Wisconsin near [here] says, 'Dean, will you come back and help our high school program?' So my first two years we won the state tournament, state championship. So I've been in coaching, whether it's development, college level, or high school level since I retired. And it's been wonderful. I have been in hockey my whole life I haven't had to grow up at all. I'm 65. I'm healthy. Yeah, life's been good."

Wayne Thomas: "I left the Sharks [as vice president and assistant general manager] the end of the '15 season to just being retired. Going to hockey rinks here and many of them in Minnesota right now. I'm at the hockey rink at seven o'clock watching my grandson play, then go back at nine-thirty watching my granddaughter play, which is a little different now. The girls are pretty high level, it's a lot of fun."

Walt Tkaczuk: "Well, I'm semi-retired, I own a golf course and a winter tube park in St. Mary's, Ontario. My daughter and my son David are running the place now and I'm just the go-fer for them, So I can wake up in the morning and have something to do. Whether I wanted to work for an hour or two hours or if I don't want to work, I don't have to do. So it's perfect for me!"

Dean Turner: "I've lived in Franklin, Michigan, in the same house for 29 or 30 years. After hockey I was out in Vancouver and I took some companies public in the resource and minerals field. I ended up settling back here in Michigan., putting together a lot of venture capital deals. Then I got involved with real estate, then mobile home parks and developed some subdivisions."

Most vivid memory of '79: "Well, being kind of on the road squad [for the Finals] where you know, wasn't gonna play, healthy scratch. They just bring a bunch of guys up, looking for next year and so you got to hang around. I remember like, after they won the first game, it was like, *Wow we can beat the Montreal Canadiens*, you can't do that. They had Guy Lafleur, Steve Shutt, Kenny Dryden, I mean on and on and on. I'd sit up there and like I'm going to be the biggest cheerleader of all, but then, of course, four straight, so that was too bad."

Steve Vickers: "I'm retired. I worked for a few businesses in New York after hockey and then I moved up to Canada some 30 years ago with a young family and worked for Bell Canada for 16 years in sales. It was a very, very good job for me and it worked out and I've been retired. I do the odd event, going down to Madison Square Garden and work part-time at a golf course in the summers. So it gets me out of the house and everything's pretty good."

His favorite memory: "I guess just, you know, beating the Flyers [in the quarterfinals]. After they beat us up in '74, that was a tough loss in seven games and that was a big one. The Islanders was a rivalry, but the Flyers was always a war, so beating them soundly like we did, that felt pretty good."

Sadly, three members of the 1978–79 Rangers have passed away, Head Coach Fred Shero in 1990, Carol Vadnais in 2014 and Greg Polis four years later.

ACKNOWLEDGEMENTS

Every book that I've written, my acknowledgments and thanks always begin with my wonderful wife, Kathy, who has been with me for nearly 40 years and the entire ride that is known as my professional career. Thanks Danny Karpin and Jake Karpin, my two young men, who Kathy and I are so proud of.

Carol and Barry Shore, my sister and her husband who have been so supportive over the years. Their children, Wendy Rosano and Sharon Shore, my wonderful nieces and my great nephew and great niece, Alex and Rachel Rosano.

Thanks to all the many friends that I've been blessed with. My longtime friends who helped me grow up, the friends who I met in college, the friends that I've met throughout my career, the friends that I've made through sports including my softball and basketball friends.

—Howie Karpin

Over my lifetime as well as the last 11 years as host of *SportstalkNy*, I must have read thousands of books. I like many others do not always take the time to read the acknowledgements. Having now gone through the process of writing four books, I have a greater appreciation as to how important these pages are to the pages that precede it, for without the names I am about to list, there would not have been a book to read.

First and foremost, as always, is my amazing wife, Beth, who is always there as an endless source of encouragement, love, and support. My son, Josh, his fiancé Stefania, and my daughter, Liana, who by the joy and passion they approach everything they do in life inspire me to do the same.

My late parents, Morris and Estelle, who allowed be to buy every sports book whenever there was a book fair at school and always encouraged me to pursue my passions.

My late sisters, Cheryl and Suzie, who always set great examples for their little brother.

I would like to thank the following members of the press who welcomed me into their work space with open arms and showed me the ropes including but not limited to Ken Albert, Christian Arnold, Matthew Blittner, Larry Brooks, Matt Calamia, Rick "Carpy" Carpinello, Jim Cerny, Scott Charles, Russ Cohen, Charles Curtis, Brett Cyrgalis, Stan Fischler, John Foyole, Bob Gelb, Zach Gelb, John Giannone, Denis Gorman, Andrew Gross, Sean Hartnett, Patrick Kearns, Allan Kreda, Don La Greca, Dave Maloney, Gil Martin, Joe McDonald, Joe Micheletti, Pat Leonard, Brian Monzo, Ira Podell, Howie Rose, Dan Rosen, Sam Rosen, Ashley Sarge, Adam Skollar, Arthur Staple, Colin Stephenson, Justin Tasch, and Steve Zipay.

Thank you to The New York Rangers PR department—John Rosasco, Ryan Nissan, Lindsay Hayes, Michael Ali, and Michael Rappaport—for all their help during this project and over the past 10 years. This project would have never happened without you. Thank you to Réjean Houle of the Montreal Canadiens Alumni Association, Karen Davis of the Columbus Blue Jackets public relations department and Wendy McCreary of the NHL Alumni Association, who were instrumental in helping me find so many former players.

Thank you to my WLIE *Sportstalkny* intern Ryan Sherman, who was a huge help in transcribing hours of interviews for this project.

A note of gratitude to the scores of authors who have appeared on WLIE 540am *Sportstalkny* who have inspired me over the years as well as our loyal sponsors Leith Baren, Neil Cohen, Robert Solomon, David and Andrew Reale, and my co-host AJ Carter as without them none of this would have been possible.

A stick tap to our editor, Ken Samelson, who allowed Howie and I to complete our hockey hat trick with him.

A special shout-out to my friends Rob Stein and Steve Kassapidis, who I shared many years of season tickets with, including the one that will last a lifetime!

Thank you to Hadley Barrett and Valerie Fabbro of The Topps Company who were instrumental in allowing to use the the 1979 Topps® trading cards on the cover ."Topps® trading cards used courtesy of The Topps Company, Inc."

Last, but not least, my writing partner in this project, Howie Karpin, as writing a book with him is like winning the Stanley Cup.

—Mark Rosenman

ABOUT THE AUTHORS

Mark Rosenman

Mark Rosenman has been covering sports in New York for almost forty years. He is currently the host and producer of Sports-Talk-NY on WLIE 540 AM. He is credentialed with the National Hockey League and Major League Baseball and covers the New York Rangers and New York Mets. With Howie Karpin, he is the co-author of Shoot to Thrill and Down on the Korner and New York Rangers by the Numbers..

Howie Karpin

Howie Karpin has been a sports reporter for more than forty years and has covered everything from the World Series to the Stanley Cup finals. He is an accredited official scorer for Major League Baseball in New York and is a contributor to Mad Dog Sports Radio, MLB Radio, and NFL Radio. With Mark Rosenman, he is coauthor of Shoot to Thrill: The History of Hockey's Shootout, Down on the Korner and Rangers by The Numbers. He lives in the Bronx, New York.

Made in the USA
Monee, IL
12 December 2020